JUDGING

TOWARDS A RATIONAL JUDICIAL PROCESS

H.J.M. BOUKEMA

JUDGING

TOWARDS A RATIONAL JUDICIAL PROCESS

1980

W.E.J. TJEENK WILLINK

Publishers

ZWOLLE - HOLLAND

The Vrije Universiteit at Amsterdam, The Netherlands, granted the degree of Doctor of Laws, based on this publication.

Dit werk diende tevens als academisch proefschrift ter verkrijging van graad van doctor in de rechtsgeleerdheid aan de Vrije Universiteit te Amsterdam waarbij als promotor optrad Prof.mr. E.J.H. Schrage en als copromotor Prof.dr. Ilmar Tammelo (Salzburg).

Library of Congres Cataloging in Publication Data

Boukema, H.J.M. 1948.
Judging: Towards a rational judicial process.
Bibliography: p. 17 includes indexes.
1. Judicial process. 2. Legal positivism. 3. Law-methodology.
1. Title.
K 213.b68 347'.01 80–18264
ISBN 90 271 1727 6

CONTENTS

Next morning Holmes knocked on the door of his father's study, "I am going to the Law School", he said without preamble. Dr. Holmes looked up from his desk. "What is the use of that?" he said. "What's the use of that, Wendell? A lawyer can't be a great man."

Yankee from Olympus
C.D. Bowen

ACKNOWLEDGEMENTS

This study is a bundle of essays collected in a book, each essay forming an integral part of the whole. Several have seen publication elsewhere, while others are due to appear shortly. The remainder of the book has been newly written.

Chapter 1.3 'Hard Theories and Hard Cases' was published in *Archives for Philosophy of Law and Social Philosophy*, A.R.S.P., Bd LXV/2 (1979), pp. 255–256.

Chapter 1.2 'Legal Realism and Legal Certainty' has been accepted for publication in the same journal.

Chapter 3.2 'Preservation of the Judiciary in the EEC' and chapter 6.3 'A Logical Scrutiny of the Van Duyn Case' has been accepted for publication in *Legal Issues of European Integration*, resp. was published there in L.I.E.I. 1978/2, pp. 83–100.

Chapter 4.3 'A Plea for the President' and chapter 5.3 'Courts and Corporations' are translations of publications in the *Nederlands Juristenblad* (Dutch Law Review) N.J.B. 79/37, pp. 847–851, resp. N.J.B. 79/29, pp. 649–654.

Chapter 6.2 'Legal Reasoning at Bar' appeared in *Rivista Internazionale di Filosofia del Diritto*, LV1–1979/2, pp. 289–296.

In particular, I should like to express my sincere thanks to Professor Ilmar Tammelo of Salzburg, Austria, who has been the most inspiring and enthusiastic force behind this study. Especially the parts on modern logic could not have been written without his help and counsel.

The friendly help and support I received from Professor E.J.H. Schrage of Amsterdam, the Netherlands, deserve special mention, particularly as our collaboration in the field of legal theory goes back to the days when I was his student in Roman Law.

I am also obliged to Professor H. Franken of Leyden, the Netherlands, for his endorsement.

It was a great encouragement when so many people responded generously to my pleas for help, advice or criticism. I must emphasize, however, that I share the blame with no one for any blemishes this study may contain. I shall not attempt to list the names of all those who helped to improve particular parts of the book, yet I feel I must single out a number of people who commented on the manuscript and whose criticism helped me to shape the material into acceptable form. Those were Mr. C.T. Barbas (Amsterdam), Mrs. E.A. Beekhuis (Bussum, the Netherlands), Mr. A. Bockwinkel (Amsterdam), Professor C.A. Boukema (Amsterdam) *il miglior fabbro*, Professor W. van Gerven (Louvain, Belgium), Professor A. Komen (Amsterdam), Dr. G.E. Langemeijer (The Hague, the Netherlands), Professor Gerald E. Lynch (New York), Mr. D.F. Murphy (Dublin, Ireland), Professor Jordan J. Paust (Houston, Texas), Professor P. van Schilfgaarde (Groningen, the Netherlands), Dr. H. Schreiner (Salzburg), Mr. S.R. Schuit (Amsterdam) and Professor H.R. Wijngaarden (Amsterdam).

I also received inestimable help from my dear friend Mrs. Cynthia J. Bennett of Pasadena, California, and of my neighbour in Amsterdam, Professor St. John Nixon of London University, each of whom read through the various drafts and took a critical look at my English.

Finally, I should like to express my appreciation and admiration to my secretary, Ingrid Mikkelsen, for her great perseverance in typing out the many drafts, and to Hedwig van Schie for her speed and efficiency in preparing the final typescript. Unfortunately, there is no one to thank for the preparation of the Index. That I had to do myself.

PROLOGUE

This study hinges upon the following assumptions.

I

The law is, in a final sense, what the judge says it is. This observation may be a truism in common law countries, but it is a relatively new concept in civil law countries, where a growing interest in the judicial decision-making process is apparent. Contemporary studies are devoted to the *way* in which the judge makes law and where limitations to do so must be imposed. Most studies originating from civil law countries explain the judicial process in legal terms only. Some, like Viehweg's *Topik und Jurisprudenz*[1] do so in an impressive manner. Other studies do rely on extra-legal explanations, but, whilst doing so, tend to be preoccupied with an introspection of the judicial process, or, in other words, with a psychology-oriented approach.

To the bewildered lawyer it is hard to adjust the prevailing theories in terms of actual experience as obtained from practicing law. (To him a theory is not true or untrue. It is useful or useless.) From the various standard works and monographic literature he would conclude that the judicial process is so complicated that, at present, it is impossible to propose one single comprehensive theory which completely covers and explains this process in all its aspects and implications.

This study dealt with some pieces of the puzzle only. Unlike most other investigations in the field it has not been written by a law professor or a judge, but by a member of the bar, who is a participating observer of the judicial process. Moreover, this study is not psychology-oriented as is the bulk of contemporary research (except, perhaps, section 5.4). On the other hand, it does not take refuge in a vicious circle to which no obviously extra-legal facts can gain admittance.[2]

Civil law countries traditionally put emphasis on making sound laws rather than on the judicial process. A typical example of this attitude is the words of Portalis, one of the drafters of the French civil code:

> De bonnes lois civiles sont le plus grand bien que les hommes puissent donner et reçevoir (. . .) elles sont (. . .) la garantie de toute paix publique et particulière; (. . .) et toujours elles font partie de sa liberté (. . .). [3]

A consequence of this way of thinking is that the legal systems of Western societies provide all the rights that the individual may need.[4] But what about their efficacy? Sound laws are fine, but there is no such thing as a self-implementing right. The individual must speak out for himself. Although all human beings are equal in the eyes of the law, some are less eloquent than others. The courts must realize this and act accordingly. Hence they should adopt a policy of judicial activism when it comes to the protection of the fundamental rights of the individual, be it against big government, big business, or big anything. Admittedly, this statement is unsophisticated. It is based upon a mistrust which is the core of the anarchist's belief: political organization based on authority is a source of all evil. Although I feel in sympathy with this belief, I am afraid that it leads nowhere.

Pericles hit the nail squarely on the head, when he defined democracy as equality before the law and political individualism (see section 3.2.2). Karl Popper updated Pericles' idea when he described the principle of democracy as the proposal to create, develop and protect political institutions for the avoidance of tyranny.[5]

II

The law safeguards the rights of the individual. The courts say what the law is, obviously playing a vital role in protecting the individual. An analysis of the judicial process is therefore relevant. But it is important to realize that the judicial process cannot be properly understood without taking into account the society in which it operates. In Western societies, the judiciary is a cornerstone of democratic government.

Chapter 1, *Democracy and Positivism*, describes this interrelation and the legal theory on which the present study is based. First and foremost, this is positivism. Where it seems appropriate, specific branches of positivism are singled out for scrutiny. Some critics may call that eclectisism or even opportunism. I prefer the term pragmatism. The controlling positivistic legal theory is the one which H.L.A. Hart propounded in his *The Concept of Law*[6], a theory that has been challenged from various quarters. An attack from outside was launched from East Berlin by Hermann Klenner, while an attack from inside the positivistic camp was launched by Ronald Dworkin from Oxford. In sections 1.2 and 1.3 respectively, I have attempted to neutralize these attacks.

III

At this stage in my exposition, it is opportune to attempt a first analysis of the judicial decision-making process. In chapter 2, *A Question of Confidence*, arguments are presented to support my contention that the outcome of court cases is not as unpredictable as many law professors and practising lawyers say it is. One sophisticated analysis of the judicial process resulted in a prediction which was accurate in 97.1% of the cases (see section 2.1.4.1). This high degree of probability, together with the means of analysing the judicial process which are offered in this study, make it possible to achieve what is usually known as legal certainty.

IV

After this analysis of how the judicial process functions the direction to which the judicial process may be headed will be scrutinized. An aspect of the relation between law and politics, more precisely the judiciary and politics, is treated in chapter 3, *A Question of Concern*. Looking at some gloomy prospects of Western Europe we cannot discount the possibility that assaults on the rights of the individual are imminent. The judiciary has the power to safeguard human rights, one of the most precious cultural inheritances of Western culture, but, in notably the EEC countries, the judiciary needs some defence mechanisms with which to ward off side-attacks.

Incidentally, in this book, the word 'politics' is used in a broad sense, while 'political' and 'moral' are used mainly in contradistinction to 'legal' (see, for instance, sections 5.1 and 5.4). Those concepts have, like all concepts of their kind, a hard core and furry edges. There is no need to define them since their meaning follows from their context. We must not be finical to a fault.

V

While the courts need some additional defence mechanism in order to help the individual, they can already do much to prevent the above mentioned assaults. In chapter 4, *A Different Viewpoint*, it is argued that, if the courts foresee the likelihood of an attack on the rights of the individual even before it takes place, they may be able to forestall it in time. In the Netherlands, for instance, public irritation with gossip publications encourages politicians to discuss curtailment of free speech. In this chapter, it is contended that the judiciary is able to mould the legal system so that it can answer the needs of contemporary society. The legislature could thus be deterred from its inclination to promulgate new laws for the curtailment of free speech. Even formalistic jurists would admit that the solution recommended in chapter 4, only appears to be *contra legem*, whereas, in fact, it is not. The grounds for justifying the courts to operate as proposed are the same indeed, as for every landmark decision where the courts make a new rule of law at a time society needs it.

VI

The point of chapters 4 and 5 is that the legal systems of Western societies are far more flexible than generally acknowledged. In chapter 5, *Discretion*, it is argued that these legal systems are flexible to such an extent that one may rightfully wonder what checks and balances they contain to guard them against becoming mere tools of judicial arbitrariness. As in chapter 4, I endeavour to make this point by scrutinizing that legal system I am most familiar with, namely, the Dutch. The limitations of judicial discretion in applying the law are outlined. They are found to be of such a nature that they effectively prevent abuse of judicial powers.

VII

Chapters 4 and 5 are of a different level or category than chapter 6. They are necessary, though, to achieve a proper understanding of the judicial process. Powerful tools to check judicial abuses are logic and 'new' rhetoric. In chapter 6, *Logic and 'New' Rhetoric*, this proposition is worked out. It cannot be said too often that modern logic is an instrument that can be used to probe the soundness of judicial reasoning, but that it does not help the process of reaching any legal decision. Only after the decision has been made can modern logic enable us to verify whether the reasoning is sound. The analysing power of modern logic is demonstrated in section 6.3, in which a decision of the Court of Justice of the European Communities is analysed and shown to be fallacious from a logical point of view. It was already one of the most criticized decisions of the Court and, in section 6.4, additional criticism is based on the logical scrutiny.

The second component of legal reasoning is the complement of logic: 'new' rhetoric or 'zetetic' (*i.e.* perduction and eduction). This component can be used among others, to make judicial decisions acceptable. As argued in section 2.1.4.4, acceptability is a crucial yardstick for evaluating and appreciating judicial decisions.

VIII

The aspects of the judicial process, as highlighted in this study, are supposed to make the judicial decision-making process transparent. Working to this goal, I have mentioned standard works and monographic literature which seemed of particular importance. No doubt some competent theorists could point out literature that I have failed to mention and which contains similar or contrary views to those I express. But this is not a reference book. Instead I have taken a look at the judicial process in my own particular way and cited only those authors whose ideas are the most catching.

Some readers may find this book helpful, others not. The reader is reminded that the philosophy of law is fraught with controversy and that the views expressed in this study might well be rejected by some competent theorists. On the other hand, I believe that other theorists would endorse the views here developed.

CHAPTER 1. DEMOCRACY AND POSITIVISM

1.1 POPPER'S APPROACH

'Democracy' is difficult to define, not only because it is vague, like so many political terms, but more importantly, because what one person would regard a paradigm case another would deny was democracy at all.[1] A perfect democracy can be found in small groups rather than in large ones. 'Precisely because democracy is a form of political organization, it must also be a pattern of leadership; nevertheless the way leaders gain and retain their authority; the extent to which their initiatives respond to the interests of those they lead; their need to listen to and answer criticism - these things distinguish a democracy in important ways'[2] from other ways of government. Although it should be acknowledged that a democratic form of government has unbecoming side-effects, the controlling assumption of this study is that it is the most appropriate of all other existing forms of government. Here no attempt will be made to define the concept of democracy. It will be taken for granted that there is a democracy, if certain characteristics are present. Some characteristics have been formulated by Karl Popper. His approach is the individualist's point of view. His approach is a modern one too. Popper wrote his *The Open Society and Its Enemies*[3] when democracies were heavily attacked by totalitarian régimes. Popper's analysis and defence of democracy give the answer to the following expression of concern:

> The belief that an indispensable constituent of a healthy democracy is a lively and politically conscious electorate; that apathy is a pathological condition, a malfunctioning of the electoral organ; that voters must be eternally vigilant to safeguard their rights and their interests against the ever-present danger of tyranny and corruption - all this has suffered rude

> shock. For, in the first place, the systems we have been accustomed to think of as the paradigms of democracy turn out not to satisfy these conditions. But even more, we are led to ask whether any system could satisfy them, given continued respect for other values, like the right to develop one's own interest free of propaganda pressure, the right of privacy, and so on. To analyze the traditional presuppositions, or norms of democratic health, in the light of our new knowledge of actual social behaviour swiftly raises the doubt whether the old model can have any relation at all to reality, whether it does not make demands which in practice are mutually incompatible.[4]

Marx underscored the significance of economic power. Contrary to Marx, Popper argues that economic power can be controlled by political power. That, in its turn can be brought under the rule of law. This can be done in democracy:

> We must think in these matters in even more materialist terms, as it were, than Marx did. We must realize that the control of physical power and of physical exploitation remains the central political problem. In order to establish this control, we must establish 'mere formal freedom'. Once we have achieved this and have learned how to use it for the control of political power, everything rests with us. We must not blame anybody else any longer, nor cry out against the sinister economic demons behind the scenes. For in a democracy, we hold the keys to the control of the demons. We can take them. We must realize this and use the keys; we must construct institutions for the democratic control of economic power, and for our protection from economic exploitation.[5]

Popper observes that what we have to guard against is an increase in the power of the rulers. We must guard against persons and their arbitrariness[6], whether these persons are private individuals or officials. Popper is wary both of unrestrained individuals and unrestrained governments. As regards the former, Popper refers to the paradox of freedom.

> Freedom, we have seen, defeats itself, if it is unlimited. Unlimited freedom means that a strong man is free to bully one who is weak and to rob him of his freedom. This is why we demand that the state should limit freedom to a certain extent, so that everyone's freedom is protected by law. Nobody should be at the *mercy* of others, but all should have a *right* to be protected by the state.[7]

With respect to governments, Popper observes:

> The individualist must maintain that the morality of states (if there is any such thing) tends to be considerably lower than that of the average citizen, so that it is much more desirable that the morality of the state should be controlled by the citizens than the opposite.[8]

Popper maintains that there are two ways of control.[9] The first is the designing of a legal framework of protective institutions. The second is that of empowering the states to act – within certain limits – as they consider necessary for achieving the ends laid down by the rulers for the time being. The preferred method is the first one, from the point of view of democratic control and that of piecemeal social engineering. Only the first, the institutional method, makes it possible to make adjustments in the light of discussion and experience. It alone makes it possible to apply the method of trial and error to our political action. Not only is this system the rational one, it is also the system that can be understood by the individual. Its functioning is predictable. It introduces a factor of certainty and security into social life.

This system works as long as citizens can freely intercourse with other citizens and that requires reason and argumentation. Reason or rationalism, says Popper,

> is an attitude of readiness to listen to critical arguments and to learn from experience. It is fundamentally an attitude of admitting that *'I may be wrong and you may be right, and by an effort, we may get nearer to the truth'*.[10]

This attitude of reasonableness is to be understood in the Socratic sense of rationalism, as opposed to the Platonic intellectual intuitionism.[11] Popper's powerful peroration for rationalism makes clear that the choice for a rationalistic approach is not an intellectual affair or a matter of taste. He insists that it is a moral decision[12], since it will deeply affect our whole attitude towards other men and towards the problems of social life.

The conclusion to be drawn from the preceding section is that, if democracy is regarded as the form of government that is worth having, a legal framework must serve to protect its purposes. This framework is to be conceived from a rationalist's point of view. Positivism is the only way of thinking that makes sense, then. After this *credo* the term 'legal positivism' needs clarification. It stands for a number of different and logically distinct doctrines.[13] In this study the term is used for referring to the doctrine that, although law and morals may often overlap or be causally related, there is not necessary or conceptual connection between them.[14] Arguably, the controversy of positivism and natural law is merely an academic one. The positivistic separation of Is and Ought must be borne in mind. But when it comes to the practice of law, the dispute seems to loose its relevance.[15] Professor Edel rightly proposes a reconsideration.[16] He submits an alternative programme, namely, pragmatic analysis:

> Clearly 'pragmatic' has to be rescued from its Nixonian sense of opportunism and from many comparable European misunderstandings. My use of it here is modest; as an analytic mode it is compatible not only with a general pragmatism but also with various forms of materialism, idealism, naturalism.[17]

Edel encourages a *craft approach* to law. He observes that crafts are altered and repatterned through the use of instruments and mechanical, electrical and biological devices. The preparation of instruments shifts from the operating craftsmen to the machine designer, and new crafts grow out of old ones as new instrumentation opens fresh possibilities.[18] If we bring this approach to the law, then the different theories may no longer come before us on proposed correct accounts of what the law really is. They are ways of looking, relative to certain methods and spurred by certain contextual interests. Some are better than others for particular purposes. Contemporary natural law theory with its method trimmed down from classical metaphysics shows how vigorous the ethical aspect of some legal phenomena is. Marxist approaches show to legal understanding the relation to social and economic developments. Edel adds:

> It may be that in given cultures and legal systems one model reads better certain parts of the law, while another other parts; or again, the legal phenomena in one society might better be described with, say, a checks-and-balances model, those in another with a bureaucratic-authority model.[19]

In this study some aspects of the judicial process will be discussed. That will be done on the basis of the assumption that a democracy needs, *inter alia*, an active judiciary in order to survive. The understanding of the judicial process, as laid down in the following chapters, may be helpful to promote the validity of this assumption. The best possible understanding of the judicial process of present Western democracies is by looking at it from the viewpoint of the positivist, by looking at it as a system of rules and distinguishing it from moral rules. The oracular theory only obscures the picture. Scrutinizing the judicial process should be done in a pragmatic manner. In the following chapters we shall freely borrow from ideas of philosophy, sociology, psychology, *etc.*. Anything that fits the analysis is acceptable.

Earlier it was submitted that the choice of a legal theory to analyze a legal system and its judiciary, is not a logical but a moral one. Hence, it must be made clear that this study will start from the concept of law as rendered by H.L.A. Hart.[20] His description of law as a system of primary and secondary rules is most illuminating. Hart's approach has been criticized, though. Two principal critics, namely Fuller[21] and Dworkin[22] go further than expressing disapproval of Hart's account in terms of a union of primary and secondary rules. They express doubts concerning the very nature of legal positivism.[23] A third kind of criticism is of a different nature. It comes from Marxist trenches and has been formulated by Klenner.[24]

The Hart-Fuller debate is well-known and here not much will be added to it. A reply to Dworkin will be offered in section 1.3, *Hard Theories and Hard Cases*. A reply to Klenner follows after the observation of the Hart-Fuller discussion. The purpose of these replies is to justify the notion of law put forward in this study as a system of primary and secondary rules. After thus securing the basic tenets of positivism, the role of the judicial officials will be dealt with in the following chapters. This will be done in the pragmatic manner as promoted by Edel, let us hope without any Nixonian backslides.

Fuller specifically disagrees with Hart's notion of the rule of recognition.[25] His standpoint is well-known and so is Hart's. The Hart-Fuller debate on the grudge informer[26] is well-known, too. It is mentioned here because it gives a case in point. A wife informed the Nazi authorities against her husband for remarks unfavourable to the régime. After the war, the woman was tried. She raised the defence that she was obliged to inform the authorities because of then existing Nazi laws. But it was established that she had made a free choice, as the law was in fact permissive, although couched in possibly imperative form. She was urged by personal and illicit motives. She was found guilty and was sentenced.

The Hart-Fuller debate was concerned with the legal justification of the decision. Hart argued that the only proper procedure in this case would have been to make criminal legislation and punishment retrospective. He contends we must choose between two evils, that of leaving the woman unpunished and that of sacrificing a precious principle of morality endorsed by most legal systems, *sc. nulla poena*. Fuller argued that a law, in order to be valid, must have an 'inner morality'. The woman was unable to refer to a valid law, since the relevant law lacked this 'inner morality'. She made sure that her husband was killed. Friedmann remarks that this conflict of view is more verbal than real.[27] In a sense, he is right. Both Hart and Fuller agree that the woman must be punished for her crime. But Hart's framing of the legal problem leaves no room for doubt about what has to be decided. Fuller's approach shifts the discussion to a meaningless and useless level: Is a morally reprehensible law a law or is it not a law? But that is not the question. Given an ethically despicable law, am I going to obey it? Once the question is framed this way, the discussion is in line. We can elaborate the conditions for civil disobedience and the like. Hart's analysis, both here and in his *The Concept of Law*, make clear that to find the proper questions is to indicate the way in which solutions may be found.

Klenner uses a method that convinces those who have the desire to become convinced, but that leaves the mind of a disinterested observer untouched. He misreads Hart's statements and then concludes they do not hold. Klenner's discourse makes clear the meaninglessness of criticizing a positivist's reasoning by measuring it against Marxist standards. Admittedly, the same would result if the reverse were attempted. To use Waismanns' words: To say that metaphysics is nonsense *is* nonsense. Here only some highlights of Klenner's writings will be annotated. Klenner insists that the first key issue of *The Concept of Law* is:

> Das *Wesen des Rechts* besteht in einer notwendigen Kombination zweier Typen sozialer Regeln, der Verpflichtungsregeln und der Befugnisübertragungsregeln.

Hart repeatedly warns that there cannot be something like the essence of law and that questions relating to that lead us nowhere.

> Die Grundlage seines Rechts liegt in einer Erkenntnisregel dieses Rechts, also das Recht ruht letztlich in sich selbst.

This is inaccurate. The rule of recognition has the character of a description of observable social behaviour. It is a matter of fact.

Klenner jests:

> Nicht einmal ein mittlerer Kleingartenverein könnte funktionieren, wenn seine Satzung nicht – in H.s. Sprache – neben Verpflichtungsregeln zugleich auch Befugnisübertragungsregeln enthielte!

Hart acknowledges that social groups of this kind may function very well.

Klenner observes:

> Dass H. zur eigentlichen Sache des Rechts also gar nicht vordringt, verdankt er seiner Forschungsmethode, die am Denkstil der (sprach-)analytischen Philosophie besonders des späten Wittgenstein, geschult und hängengeblieben ist.

The words 'eigentliche Sache des Rechts' are meaningless.

Klenner concludes:

> H.S 'Begriff des Rechts' belegt, dass das sprachanalytische Vorgehen innerhalb der juristischen Grundlagenforschung sich auch in H.s kluger Handhabung als ungeeignet erweist, das Recht auf seinen Begriff zu bringen

Clearly, there is a divergence of opinions here. In the Western world at least, it is widely recognized that Hart's legal theory does enable us to grasp the nature of a legal system and hence obtain an adequate understanding of the concept of law. Hart's approach is a sophisticated one. He has employed the methods of analytical philosophy and logical positivism. These methods are incompatible with the views of a staunch Marxist like Klenner. Positivism and metaphysics are hard to reconcile. The purpose of mentioning Klenner's criticism is not to demonstrate that Hart is right and Klenner is wrong. Positivists already think so and those who agree with Klenner will remain unimpressed. The purpose is rather to emphasize that one simply has to adopt one method and employ it. If the selected method works, the choice is good. In this study Hart's method is embraced. I find that this method illuminated the legal system and the concept of law. Due to Hart's analysis I have an improved understanding of the judicial process. Marxist dogmas or any metaphysical system for that matter, do not clarify anything. There is no point in reaping with a sickle, when a combined harvester is available. The combined application of positivist and pragmatic methods is the way to pursue an analysis of the judicial process in Western societies.

1.3.1 Introduction

Ronald M. Dworkin, a legal philosopher of American origin, who holds the chair of jurisprudence at Oxford, has launched an attack on legal positivism.[28] His attack is powerful. He has located seemingly brittle components of positivism with lucid reasoning. He claims that standards make positivism untenable. He offers his rights thesis to explain the role of standards. This article contains a refutation of Dworkin's 'hard theories' and it makes plain that standards are consistent with positivism.

1.3.2 Dworkin's Suppositions

In the chapter *The Model of Rules I*[29] Dworkin states the key tenets of positivism as follows[30]:

a. The law of a community is a set of special rules used by the community directly or indirectly for the purpose of determining which behavior will be punished or coerced by the public power. These special rules can be identified and distinguished by specific criteria, by tests having to do not with their content but with their *pedigree* or the manner in which they were adopted or developed. These tests of pedigree can be used to distinguish valid legal rules from spurious legal rules (rules which lawyers and litigants wrongly argue are rules of law) and also from the other sorts of social rules (generally lumped together as 'moral rules') that the community follows but does not enforce through public power.

b. The set of these valid legal rules is exhaustive of 'the law', so that if someone's case is not clearly covered by such a rule (because there is none that seems appropriate, or those that seem appropriate are vague, or for some other reason) then that case cannot be decided by 'applying the law'. It must be decided by some official, like a judge, exercising his discretion, which means reaching beyond the law for some other sort of standard to guide him in manufacturing a fresh legal rule or supplementing an old one.

c. To say that someone has a 'legal obligation' is to say that his case falls under a valid legal rule that requires him to do or to forbear from doing something. (To say he has a legal right, or has a legal power of some sort, or a legal privilege or immunity, is to assert, in a shorthand way, that others have actual or hypothetical legal obligations to act or not to act in certain ways touching him.) In the absence of such a valid legal rule there is no legal obligation; it follows that when the judge decides an issue by exercising his discretion, he is not enforcing a legal obligation as to that issue.

These suppositions will be looked at first.

ad 1: A positivist uses formal criteria to identify a legal rule. He does not look at the content of a legal rule to decide whether the rule is a legal one. Dworkin is right when he attributes this proposition to positivism.

ad 2: Dworkin is incorrect when he says that if someone's case is not clearly covered by a rule, that case cannot be decided by 'applying the law'. To apply the law implies interpretation of the relevant rules, to weigh the interests of the plaintiff against those of the defendent, to select the relevant facts, to take into consideration the logic of the legal systems and its aims, etc. If the court is unable to apply the law, it is not competent to decide the case. Dworkin's notion of discretion will be discussed later (see section 1.3.5).

ad 3: Dworkin's description of the positivist doctrine is not accurate. It is incorrect to say that when the judge decides an issue by exercising his discretion, he is not enforcing a legal obligation on that issue. Exercising his discretion implies the interpretation of a legal rule and the subsumption of the case under that rule. Exercising discretion is part of applying the law. If a judge decides a case and if his final decision meets all (formal) demands of the legal system, it is the law. Again, the concept of discretion will be dealt with later. A judge is not deciding a legal issue properly if the reasoning that leads to his decision is inconsistent and cannot be traced down to existing legal rules. Such a decision does not enforce a legal right and an appeal against it will be successful. If there is no legal obligation on the one hand and no legal right on the other, the court is not competent.

Dworkin's suppositions in his attack on positivism do not hold and it will be argued that the remainder of his reasoning is debatable as well.

1.3.3 Standards

Dworkin attacks positivism. He argues[31] that it is a model of and for a system of rules, and that its central notion of a fundamental test for law forces us to miss the important roles of the standards, principles and policies that are not rules. Dworkin calls a *policy* that kind of standard that sets out a goal to be reached, generally aiming at an improvement in some economic, political or social feature of the community. He calls a *principle* a standard that is to be observed, not because it will advance or secure an economic, political or social situation deemed desirable, but because it is a requirement of justice or fairness or another dimension of morality.

It is not clear what Dworkin means with 'to miss the important roles of standards.' His clarification with the help of renowned hard cases is insufficient. A hard case is at stake when a particular lawsuit cannot be brought under a clear rule of law laid down by some institution in advance.[32] Dworkin concludes that in some cases there is no (clear) rule and that the court renders its decision by applying standards that are not legal rules. He claims that positivism stops short of just those puzzling hard cases that send us looking for the theories of law.

According to Dworkin's definition of a hard case, a judge has to deal with a large number of hard cases, which he does not consider to be very hard. From the facts that are presented to him by both the parties involved, the judge selects the (legally) relevant facts and tries to subsume them under a legal rule. When the judge fails to find an applicable legal rule covering the selected facts and when rearrangements of the facts do not produce better results, the judge has to conclude that he is not competent to decide the case. This does not happen very often. The bulk of important legal rules are not clear in the sense Dworkin means. Most legal rules require some kind of interpretation before they can be applied.

The skill of a judge consists in his ability to select the relevant facts to interprete the legal rules.

Dworkin does, however, have a valid point as far as he attracts attention to the role of standards. But standards are not applied as if they were legal rules and they are not inconsistent with positivism. Later this statement will be developed, but first Dworkin's solution for the alleged embarrassment of the positivist will be discussed.

1.3.4 The Rights Thesis

Dworkin offers his *rights thesis*. As stated by theory, judicial decisions enforce existing political rights:

> Judges, like all political officials, are subject to the doctrine of political responsibility. This doctrine states, in its most general form, that political officials must make only such political decisions as they can justify within a political theory that also justifies the other decisions they propose to make.[33]

And what an enforceable political right is, is decided by a political theory:

> Political rights are creatures of both history and morality: what an individual is entitled to have, in civil society, depends upon the practice and the justice of its political institutions.[34]

The word 'political' is vague. It would be hard to sharply distinguish between political theories, religious theories, philosophical theories and moral theories. To an equal degree it is hard to discern a series of politically coloured thoughts from a political theory. Most judges would reject the suggestion that they have political responsibility 'like all political officials.' They would consider it unfair to have thrust upon them a responsibility without being granted a proportional and related competence.

Unless the concept of 'political' is stretched to cover all acts of all officials at any time, it is meaningless to attribute to a judge political responsibility 'like all political officials'. Some judicial decisions have political consequences. A legal system contains rules that formulate political goals and by applying the law the courts enforce these goals. But that does not justify Dworkin's dogma. A Secretary of State, a Member of Parliament, a municipal council etc. bear political responsibility. A judge does not. Dworkin fails to show the way out of the dilemma when conflicting political theories, backing incompatible 'existing rights' are presented to the court. If Dworkin really supports the idea that a judge might have to decide this dilemma, he confuses a courtroom for Hyde Park Corner. This rights thesis leads nowhere, and tells nothing. Dworkin rightly observes that hard cases send us to look at legal theory, but his rights thesis is a dead-end street.

Dworkin is disarming when he confesses that, also in hard cases, one party has the right to win and that there are not definite criteria to find out which party is the lucky one (Hart criticizes this in *Georgia Law Review*[35]). This confession is also a testimony of weakness, though. He cannot claim to build a model 'truer to the complexity and sophistication of our own practices'[36] and offer nothing better than his political rights thesis. Dworkin came to this theory while being concerned about the alleged sneaking out of the positivist when in a hard case a judge begs legal theorists for help. The rights thesis does not help the poor judge who has no tools to find out which of two parties has a *right* to win. The losing party might be outraged: *he* has a *right* to win and why does he not get what he is entitled to.

It does more justice to 'the complexity and sophistication of our practice' to say that both parties have their rights, but that one party has *better* rights, or has better claims to rights, or is able to have his rights better displayed, and that he must win for that reason. The judge must give a fair, that is, impartial and objective judgment. He must give his decision and the reasoning supporting his decision in such a way that both parties understand that their arguments and claims have been scrutinized and weighed. The balance of pros and cons must be in favour of the winning party. The losing party may appeal to the supreme court. And the final decision is the law.

People's claims cannot be called 'rights' when there is only a political theory backing them up. A political theory must be adopted by a political party, which incorporates it into a political programme. If the party is in office it has eventually a chance to result into law. Until then it remains theory. Take for instance the case that inhabitants of houseboats demand to be linked in with electricity and natural gas, but the community council and the electricity and natural gas companies refuse this demand. Suppose further the houseboat inhabitants cannot mention any statute to their support, but that they have a sound political theory backing their claims. In addition, they can give a great number of examples in which the authorities gave way to similar demands and there is a general feeling in the country that houseboat dwellers should not be deprived of the benefits of electricity and natural gas. If the courts are unable to link a decision in favour of the houseboat residents to the legal system by means of sound reasoning, they will refuse to rule that the local government and the companies involved should provide the plaintiffs with electricity and natural gas. Then the houseboat inhabitants have no *right* to be linked in, in spite of their political theory. The newspapers may launch a campaign in favour of the water dwellers and at protest meetings everybody may sympathize with them, but the losers of the lawsuit have no *right* worth mentioning. Someone has a right when the legal system provides for it and one is able to enforce his rights if the courts are co-operative.

1.3.5 Discretion

Some legal philosophers argue that in cases where no clear rule dictates the solution, the judge must exercise his discretion. Dworkin attacks this idea. He says that '(d)iscretion, like the hole in a doughnut, does not exist except as an area left open by a surrounding belt of restriction. It is therefore a relative concept'[37].

Dworkin is right there, but his distinction between discretion in a weak sense and in a strong sense, and his conclusions from this distinction do not stand criticism. If a sergeant is ordered to take his five most experienced men to patrol,

Dworkin grants him discretion in a weak sense. Discretion in the strong sense in Dworkin's words is when there are no standards set by the authority in question. In this sense Dworkin says that a sergeant who has been told to pick any five men for patrol he chooses uses discretion. The authority in question did, however, set standards for the sergeant. The sergeant was to take five men on patrol, no more and no less.

The words 'weak' and 'strong' are confusing. In either case the range of the discretion is an area left open by a belt of restriction. In one case the area is somewhat larger than in the other. The positivist, who ascribes discretion to the judge, presumes that the judge works within a legal system, and has the option of applying the law in several ways. The judge is not competent to go outside the legal system. He cannot run out of rules. In this sense the judge *always* uses discretion to some extent, since it is his job to select the facts, to find the rule and to apply it. Dworkin calls this point of view the nominalist's and denies it to be the positivist's. Here he only calls names and evades the objections against this theory.

Judges always have some degree of discretion when they apply the law. They are restricted by the legal system. The proof whether their decisions are in harmony with the legal system lies in the soundness of the argumentation of the judgment. Modern logic can help us to check the consistency of the reasoning. Our understanding of the structure of the legal system at hand enables us to check whether the decision is in harmony with the legal system. It goes without saying that a logical judicial decision has to meet some more criteria before we consider it to be an understandable and good decision.

A problem has to be faced when a judgment implies a new policy of the court. From time to time the court abandons a doctrine and sets up a new one. This is, however, hardly a theoretical problem, but a matter of fact. The question how far a court may go is not for the philosopher to describe. The end of the court's tether is outlined by society itself. A legal system contains provisions to ensure that the courts do not break the law. There is an area, though, that cannot be covered by the law. For example the integrity and morality of supreme court justices is the last guarantee that they do not twist or bend the law but follow the constitution. In some countries the fear of government intervention keeps the courts in line and in Western countries the legislator keeps an eye on them. If the court trespasses, it causes a political problem. The officials should realize that the bulk of the rules must be habitually obeyed by a large majority of the people. There is a limited amount of behaviour that the law can enforce. The efficacy of a legal system depends mainly on its acceptance by the citizens and not upon the power of its enforcement. This holds for a democracy and a constitutional state. I leave aside a totalitarian regime that rules by terror and intimidation. A legal system can flourish only when the officials do not estrange themselves from the public. Of course, in every legal system the courts make mistakes and make bad decisions, either morally or technically. A legal system is able to absorb a number of mistakes but it is difficult to decide by means of a legal theory how many.

An attempt to solve this problem has been made by the Viennese legal theorist Adolf Merkl[38]. This attempt shows *inter alia* that it is impossible to point out how many mistakes are necessary for a legal system to collapse. Legal systems are not without gaps, except in cases, where they obtain a closure principle (such as: 'Whatever is legally not prohibited is legally permitted'), in which cases *non-liquet* declarations are possible for the courts. When the court is faced with an apparent gap it may either declare itself not authorized or deal with the matter with standards of, say, justice and reasonableness. The question remains how far the court may stretch the legal rule to fill the gap. I shall try to give a theoretical answer to this question in the succeeding paragraphs. Each judicial decision is also scrutinized on its practical merits: is it acceptable? That question comes after the conclusion that the decision meets all the formal criteria of the legal system.

1.3.6 The Is and the Ought

H.L.A. Hart, Dworkin's predecessor at Oxford, argues in his *Concept of Law*[39] that the phenomenon law can only be understood when we look at rules concerning human behaviour, especially rules of obligation. Not all such rules are legal rules and Hart rightly observes that legal rules are to be distinguished from all other kind of rules by one characteristic: they are framed in a system of primary and secondary rules. The latter are rules of the second degree, *viz.* rules about rules. Consequently, law is always to be understood in a legal system of primary and secondary rules. Hart's *The Concept of Law* has eliminated a number of issues that for centuries vexed and alarmed philosophers. It is deplorable that Dworkin tries to backslide into the darkness of natural law, that fails to distinguish between the Is and the Ought. With the help of *The Concept of Law* we are able to distinguish between a valid legal rule and a spurious one and between an existing valid legal rule and a non-existing rule.

Finally, a valid and existing legal rule may be morally wrong to an extent that one does not acknowledge its binding force. It is useless and misleading to say that a valid rule is invalid because it does not meet certain moral standards. The purpose of this reasoning is to supply a justification for not obeying such a rule. It is unnecessary to follow the detour of denying the qualification 'legal' to such a rule. It is understood that not all legal rules are always binding. Every sophisticated legal system contains exceptions to the binding force of legal rules. And one's sense of morality adds more exceptions. It is dangerous to give the concepts of 'law' and of 'legal' such a lofty connotation that only morally impeccable legal rules are to be called legal rules. Many atrocities were justified by the law. Mankind is better served if such a justification meets the remark: 'So what? The law is wrong then! And I am not going to obey it.' It is far too scholastic to demand a moral minimum content of the law and to conclude that a legal rule is not legal if it is not a moral rule as well. Once more we come to see that Dworkin's theory blurs the distinction between law and morals.

1.3.7 The Role of Standards

Dworkin deservedly calls attention to the role of standards. Standards are important for the judge. They are his guidelines in interpreting and applying the law. Standards are instructions for embarking on a course. They are regulative ideas. They are like lighthouses guiding a judge in understanding and interpreting legal rules. After the judge has found his way through the case at bar and has decided which party should win, and why, he uses standards as a matter of reference and justification.

Standards may be framed in the same way as rules are. A tenet such as the *nullum crimen, nulla poena sine lege* is a legal rule when it has been incorporated in a penal code and has thus lost its status of standard. The important difference between legal rules and standards is that the former are definitely a part of a legal system. The status of standards in relation to a legal system is doubtful. There is a wide range of standards. Some are merely technical. For example: how to deliver a judgment, how to use words, how to use references. Some standards are rather vague such as the concept of formal justice: 'To each member of the same class, the same,' or the precepts of material justice, such as: 'To each according to his needs,' or 'To each according to his merits.' Some standards are moral: 'No one shall be permitted to take advantage of his own wrong.' The courts sometimes make use of standards expressed rhetorically: 'Is there any principle which is more familiar or more firmly embedded in the history of Anglo-American law than the basic doctrine that the courts will not permit themselves to be used as instruments of inequity and injustice?'.

Dworkin insists that 'positivism, on its own thesis, stops short of just those puzzling hard cases that send us to look for theories of law'[40]. This statement is doubtful. If Dworkin is perplexed by the role of standards in judicial decision, he might compare the law-making process of the judge and that of the legislator. It is the legislator's task to create new law. It is the judge's task to apply the law, not to create it. Some positivists contend that the judge always creates law when he is applying law. Natural-law believers deny this and say that it is up to the judge to *find* the law, not to create it. This is also Dworkin's opinion. According to a philosophical theory of spatial-temporal locations, everything is always unique. In this sense of uniqueness, the judge always creates law.

This concept of uniqueness is not helpful. In most cases the judge applies the law in the same manner each time and it is pointless to say that he is creating new law. In some cases the judge gives a new interpretation of applicable rules and applies these in a new manner. One could say that this is creating new law. The judge may even take into account the same standards as the legislator would have taken, were he dealing with the matter. The judge tries to operate within the legal system and to make his decision consistent with the system. The legislator, of course, also operates within a legal system. But he is free to abandon rules and create fully new rules that are inconsistent with the abandoned ones. The legislator creates rights, liberties and restrictions. Judicial decisions may have the same effect. The question arises as to what the difference is between a legislator and a court. There are formal and obvious differences. In addition, it must be observed that the *trias politica doctrine* à la Montesquieu does not hold all the time.

Again, the standards that are guides to the members of parliament when passing a new bill, may be the same as the ones the judge uses. But the judge is not supposed to run out of rules and he ought to link his decision to the legal system by means of sound reasoning, that is, reasoning that is convincing and acceptable. If the judge fails to attach the content of his decision to the legal system, he sees to it that its form looks like that of his other decisions. In this way the judge may create new law. It is law if it cannot be challenged. This practice is as old as judicial practice. It is judicial practice. Here remains the question of how far and how often the judge can afford to break out of the restrictions of his legal system. And here lies the great difference between a legislator and a court. The legislator is much freer to abandon old rules and to create new ones. The judge uses standards as justification for his interpretation or stretching of legal rules. Standards have the role of improving the acceptability of judicial decisions. They are not a source of law as the rights thesis pretends.

The legislator does not need the justification that its latest decision is consistent with previous ones. The legislator is entitled to deprive groups of their prerogatives and transfer these to others. The judge is not supposed to do so. A judge applies the law and tries to operate within the scope of a legal system. He sometimes trespasses either out of ignorance or when he feels obliged to do so. Dworkin is right when he insists that the judge should follow principles and not policies. But the distinction between the two is not always clear.

1.3.8 Court Rhetoric

Standards are references explaining the train of thought the court has followed. They are also references criticizing the court's decisions. A judicial decision must be a good decision. The word 'good' means both morally good and legally or technically good. The decisions must be fair, that is, it must show that the arguments of the parties involved have been understood and appreciated. The decision must make clear why the arguments are accepted or rejected. The judgement must be consistent with the previous decisions or must give a satisfactory explanation of why the court altered its course.

Modern logic in the service of law helps to determine which premises in judicial arguments are *logically* necessary as a base for the conclusion. All the other arguments are *logically* redundant. They may be requested for another reason. The officials must see to it that they do not estrange themselves from their citizens. They ought to make their decisions acceptable to them (and to their fellow-lawyers). In order to do so, the logically redundant premisses are rhetorically called for to convince all who are concerned that the case was decided in the best way. Standards are a means of appreciating the rhetorical argument *per analogiam*. Analogy is logically inconclusive, but the courts use it to do justice to the standard: treat equal cases alike.

U.S. courts have the commendable tradition of elaborating their reasons for rendering their decisions. They try to give decisions that are clear to the intelligent layman and not only to other lawyers. This practice is to be understood as an attempt to improve the acceptability of judicial decisions.

The above outline of the role of standards fits into a positivist's description of law. The existence of standards does not force us to leave the positivist doctrine of the separation of legal and moral rules.

1.3.9 Conclusion

It is to Dworkin's credit that he highlights the role of standards in judicial decision-making. He is wrong, though, when he argues that positivism does not give a satisfactory explanation for this role. Moreover, he is wrong when he concludes that legal positivism has to be rejected. He disregards the attainment of positivism, notably the 'separation' (or rather the differentiation) of the legal and moral universes of discourse. Dworkin points out that the positivist's explanation of the role of standards is unsatisfactory, but to say good-bye to positivism for that reason is to cut off one's nose to spite one's face.

This chapter criticizes the core of the rights thesis, namely, if two parties come to court, one has a *right* to win, but there is no way to discover which party that is. The rights thesis with its background rights, institutional rights, policies and principles is a nice and attractive theory. It reminds one of 19th century German idealistic philosophy. When one of its zealots was told that his theory was incompatible with the facts, he retorted: 'That's too bad for the facts, then'. Dworkin appeals to a lawyer's wildest dreams: Every case has but one solution; no one would have to go to court anymore. Unfortunately, his rights thesis is not 'a model truer to the complexity and sophistication of our own practices'[41]. And lawsuits will be pending.

1.4 STANDARDS: A CATEGORY-MISTAKE

In paragraph 1.3 the role of standards was described. This section attempts, in a probably vain effort to persuade those who stubbornly remain unconvinced. Usually their line of thought goes as follows. If the courts use standards when they decide a case, they use standards as a source of law. Rules are a source of law and if standards are the same, what is the difference?

Law is what the courts say it is. Judicial decisions are the law, then. Which ingredients do the judges use to render a decision? They use words, paper and ink. In short, they use empirical data of a non-legal nature. These ingredients are necessary for the law. Are they a source of law? Bias, predilections and prejudices of the judge are an innate ingredient of the law. Are they a source of law? Political considerations loom in the art of adjudicating and, according to Cardozo, the forces that singly or in combination shape the making of the law are logic, history, custom and utility.[42] Are they sources of law? The facts determine the outcome of a case, too. Are they sources of law? More questions like these can be asked.

The reason why of all these sources of law only standards are sometimes considered to be of the same standing as legal rules is that standards are phrased in the arcane language of legal rules. But to be misled by that use of language is to give way to *category-mistakes*. This concept is explained by Gilbert Ryle in his *The Concept of Mind*.[43] Here one of Ryle's examples will be repeated:

> A foreigner watching his first game of cricket learns what are the functions of the bowlers, the batsmen, the fielders, the umpires and the scorers. He then says 'But there is no one left on the field to contribute the famous element of team-spirit. (...) Once more, it would have to be explained that he was looking for the wrong type of thing. Team-spirit is not another cricketing-operation supplementary to all of the other special tasks. It is, roughly, the keenness with which each of the special tasks is performed, and performing a task keenly is not performing two tasks.

Often standards are a way of describing court behaviour. If counsel wishes to arrange the best position for his client, he should ensure that his client goes to court 'with clean hands'. The courts like that. If two litigants have equally strong claims, the courts may give the benefit of the doubt to the litigant with clean hands. Dworkin gives an example of another legal principle or standard.[44] He quotes a New Jersy court indulging in rhetorical exclamations:

> Is there any principle which is more familiar or more firmly embedded in the history of Anglo-American law than the basic doctrine that the courts will not permit themselves to be used as instruments of inequity and injustice?

Contrary to Dworkin's opinion, this declaration of the courts does not warrant the conclusion that standards are of the same standing as legal rules. The court discloses its frame of mind according to which it will perceive and interpret the applicable legal rule. Sometimes, judges too can be misled by the rule-like appearance of standards.

As explained further in section 7.3, *A Logical Scrutiny of the Van Duyn Case*, the judge should see that his decision is attached to the legal system by means of logical sound reasoning. If the judge uses a standard not in a 'rhetorical sense' in order to improve the acceptability of his judgment, but as a logically necessary premiss, he renders logically unsound reasoning. When such a decision stands in a final sense, it is the law. *That* decision is later a precedent and a source of law. It is then incorporated in the legal system. If the judge's lack of logic makes standards convert into legal rules, this is no reason to conclude that the positivist's distinction between Is and Ought is obsolete.

1.5 TWO MAIN QUESTIONS RELATING TO LAW

When one is confronted with the law, two main questions become apparent. Those who do not look at the law in incurious wonder repeat these questions from time to time. Gradually the answers change. They may show more knowledge and insight. The first question is, of course, *What is the law?* In this study it is assumed that H.L.A. Hart in his *The Concept of Law* has adequately dealt with this question. In paragraph 1.2 a clarification is given of the paramount importance of Hart's analysis.

The second question will be the theme of chapter 2. It is a question that enters into the mind of anyone who takes up legal practice. After being taught by law school professors, the young lawyer meets clients, who tell him about their problems and how they want them to be solved. He then has the task of trying to achieve that result. That is an appalling experience. Our young lawyer will have to make up his mind as to *what the courts would do*? There is the second question. In this study, it is assumed that the Legal Realists have shown how to deal with this question. They have fully appreciated the vital role of the judge in law-making.

Our Western societies are being transformed and their legal systems are being renewed. The reconstruction is largely done by the courts. Where the law-giver remains inert, the judges assume responsibility. A case in point is the well-known *High-Trees* case.[45] Lord Denning, who was involved in this judicial performance, gives inside information in *The Discipline of Law*.[46] It is the controlling conviction of this book that an understanding of the judicial process is required for both the bar and the bench, in order to keep step with the transformation of the law. Perhaps it would be easy if the dreams of Frederick the Great or Napoleon were true: legal disputes can be settled by strictly applying the Code. But these dreams never came true. Jerome Frank discussed this desire for certainty and uniformity[47]:

> Where, then, is the hope for complete uniformity, certainty, continuity in law? It is gone except to the extent that the personalities of all judges will be substantially alike, to the extent that the judges will all have substantially identical mental and emotional habits. And here we come to a curious conclusion: it is perhaps just possible that we could get stereotyped results from our judges by picking stereotyped men for the judicial office. If we were to elect or appoint to the bench the most narrow-minded and bigoted members of the community, selected for their adherence to certain relatively fixed and simple prejudices, willing to be and remain ignorant of those niceties of difference between individuals the apprehension of which makes for justice, and insensitive to the rate of social change - we then might have stability in law. There is little hope of such stability, however, if our judges are the more enlightened, sensitive, intelligent members of the community, for then there will be small likelihood that all judges will react identically to a given set of unique facts, in particular legal controversies. In a deeper sense, however, uniformity of point of view among judges is likely to increase to the extent that judges are the more enlightened, the more quick to detect and hold in check their own prejudices, the more alive to the fact that rules and precedents are not their masters but merely agencies to be utilized in the interest of doing justice.

Frank's observation is still valid, but the development of the techniques of political scientists, psychologists and sociologists enables them to be more helpful than was possible in Frank's day. An up-to-date view on the judicial process will be offered in chapter 2. To understand the judges who make the law is to understand the law. In the next chapter, this understanding will be developed in relation to an important issue, namely, legal certainty. Ideally, the law is both stable and flexible. Today quite a number of lawyers complain that judicial renewal may be fine, but that legal certainty is diminishing to an alarming degree. But whose fault is that? That of a volatile bench or their own?

CHAPTER 2. A QUESTION OF CONFIDENCE

2.1 LEGAL REALISM AND LEGAL CERTAINTY

2.1.1 Introduction

The term 'Legal Realism' covers a variety of ways of looking at the law.[1] These ways share a hostility towards the oracular theory[2] and focus on a theory of judging. Legal Realism assumes that judging can be an illogical, idiosyncratic exercise as is any other form of human decision-making.[3] It has been particularly concerned with reducing the uncertainty that necessarily results from irrational aspects of judicial decision-making and has tried to achieve its aims through empirical observation resulting in methods of predicting court decisions. These days few jurists, if any, call themselves Legal Realists. Still there is widespread concern among practicing lawyers with respect to the Realists' cherished theme, namely, the unforeseeable outcome of court cases. For this and other reasons, many competent lawyers are reluctant to advise their client to submit his case to the court and prefer to try to settle matters. It is laudable to solve problems that way. It is, however, disquieting if the urge to do so is caused by the belief that the judiciary is unreliable and that one can hardly tell the outcome of a case at bench by recourse to methods of legal reasoning.

In this section it is contended that this feeling of uncertainty[4] is not primarily caused by inadequate performance of the judicature. On the contrary, it reflects an unsophisticated perception of the nature of the judicial process. Some precepts of Legal Realism will be updated to illustrate this point. Then the concept of 'legal certainty' will be discussed. Finally, aspects of the nature of the judicial decision-making process will be scrutinized. Professor Bickel spoke of the 'arrested realists'[5], since the realists would only consider the outcome of a case, not the process. If so, this study is an example of 'released realism', since it not only considers the outcome of a case, but also the decision-making process.

2.1.2 The Movement up to the Present

Legal Realism has been a prominent mode of legal thinking in the New World. Its roots can be traced far back in the history of Western philosophy.[6] There has not been, strictly speaking, a school of Realists.[7] New recruits of the movement required tools and stimuli; old adherents diverged in interests from each other. They had in common an interest in the 'law in action' at courts. They did not forget that an important contribution to a legal system was offered by the lawgivers. Nor did they ignore the vast area of application of the law situated outside the courtroom.[8] But they focused their attention on legal decision-making by the courts. A question of paramount interest to the Legal Realists is: What would the court do? After all, the court's attitude about a legal matter is what counts. If the court does not enforce the law, the law might be a dead letter. Every practicing lawyer knows that one can only tell what the law is when one knows how the court applies it. Mr Justice Holmes has put it most eloquently in his address *The Path of the Law*.[9] This speech was delivered in 1897; its relevance is still obvious.

> The object of our study, then, is prediction, the prediction of the incidence of the public force through the instrumentality of the courts (...) If you want to know the law and nothing else, you must look at it as a bad man, who cares only for the material consequences which such knowledge enables him to predict, not as a good one, who finds his reasons for conduct, whether inside the law or outside of it, in the vaguer sanctions of conscience. (...) But if we take the view of our friend the bad man we shall find that he does not care two straws for the axioms or deductions, but that he does want to know what the Massachusetts or English courts are likely to do in fact. I am much of his mind. The prophecies of what the courts will do in fact, and nothing more pretentious, are what I mean by the law.

Variations on this theme have been made by other Realists, some while underscoring the importance of the legal decision-making process, others by emphasizing its impact on court decisions.[10] A number of significant observations prevailing among Legal Realists will be dealt with briefly.

Realists found it remarkable that, even if the language of a statute is crystal clear, the outcome of a court case is always more or less uncertain.[11] As a result Realists studied the nature of the judicial process. They disclosed that the chief obstacle to prophesying a trial court decision is the inability – thanks to factors they deemed inscrutable – to foresee what a particular trial judge (or jury) will believe to be the relevant facts (hereinafter some 'inscrutable' factors will be discussed). The trial court may frame a case at bench quite differently from the one the litigants have in mind. On appeal, the court usually gives a decision based on the case as it is put at trial court level. *Fact scepticism*, then, tends to pay attention to this cause of legal uncertainty. There is also *rule scepticism*. The merits of that way of thinking come to light especially at upper court level, but it also intertwines with the trial court stage. Rule scepticism contends that one cannot fully anticipate which rule the court will deem to be applicable and, moreover, which interpretation the court will give to a rule it considers to be applicable.[12]

One may assume that fact scepticism explains the source of legal uncertainty at trial court level, whereas rule scepticism gradually does this while the case develops to upper court level.[13] This rough bipartition holds when we presume that the trial court is more bound, than binding; that it has no superior authority; that it is obliged to statutes and the body of experienced law; that most legal matters presented before its bench are already settled although many are not.

Many philosophers tried to determine what a *fact* is. The only certain result is disagreement. But what a court says that the relevant facts are may sometimes surpass comprehension. What the court regards as a fact is what it determines to be a fact for the purpose of law. It may happen to be a non-fact in the realm of empirical science. Only if the court finds it virtually impossible to conclude its reasoning, must it change its mind and give judgment for the other party. The court is seldom confronted with such a situation. Fact scepticists also point out that a lawyer cannot know in advance exactly how a witness will give testimony or which evidence the other party will offer. A lawyer can only try to investigate one side of the case. How successful he is in discovering the facts that are available to him depends, *inter alia*, on how he perceives the case. Psycholegal research by Thibaut and Walker[14] makes it clear that, if a lawyer is determined to win his case, but knows he represents the weaker side, he is much more effective in fact-finding than when he is confident in having a cast-iron case.

Besides this uncertainty relating to facts, there is the truism that the meaning of legal rules varies as time passes. The open texture of legal concepts and, for that matter, legal rules, has been illuminated by H.L.A. Hart.[15] Recently R.M. Dworkin[16] highlighted that a *concept* has many *conceptions*. Conceptions reflect the perception of a concept. Hence a rule from 1880 can hardly be the same in 1980. This explains the capacity of adaptation of a legal system to changed conditions. It also clarifies the innate characteristic of growth and the development of legal concepts and, consequently, of a legal system. After a period of time, one can describe where and when the courts switched their policy and formed new rules. It is difficult for a lawyer to predict when that change will take place.

Judicial innovation is sometimes called for in order to do justice. From this perspective, judicial innovation occasionally clashes with the value of the predictability of judicial decisions. When economic, social or political circumstances change, one would like the law to change proportionally and gradually. But law-givers often forsake their duties. The judiciary has to wait for a case at bench before it can take action. This, and the fact that the judicature has the power to declare, in final sense, what 'the law is', are causes for the spasmodic growth of the law. The prediction of the outcome of court cases may be especially difficult in those cases where the court is asked to rule in a matter of political controversy. In such cases, the courts help to govern the country, being a counter-majoritarian force in our society.[17] Management or government by the courts has the advantage that it is done by reasonably competent persons who are not as vulnerable to political pressure as those belonging to the other branches of public authority. Hence the courts are able to protect the individual against 'big government'. These activities imply a policy of the courts and that, in its turn, causes another hurdle for predicting court cases.

The above outline suggests that many factors influence the outcome of the judicial decision-making process. How could one ever think that the result of this flux could be predicted *with certainty*?

Legal Realists acknowledged that lawyers advise their clients as to the probable forms of judicial behaviour. Some Realists emphasized the great influence of personality, prejudice and other non-rational factors upon the making of the law. The prejudice of the judge may be racial, religious, political or economic. His bias may also be hidden. One could think that litigants would like to have access to the judge's psychograms or to his records of psycho-analysis, if any. It is unlikely that such wishes will ever be fulfilled. One cannot but empathize with the lawyer who maintains that law is what the judge had for breakfast. The personality of the decision-maker is a source of uncertainty. An experienced lawyer will, however, be able to reduce the amount of uncertainty. It is obvious for anyone who attends a court day, where the bar and the bench know each other well, that there may be an invisible link between them, so that some communion of feeling is established.[18] Probably neither party would be capable of explaining what it is. Let us call it 'experience' or 'expertise' of those who work in the vicinity of the bench.

The makers of the law are not only influenced by the factors of their human personality, but also by those of social environment, economic conditions, business interest, current ideas and popular emotion.[19] Legal Realists felt free to turn to psychologists, sociologists and the like in an effort to clarify the judicial process. Unlike believers of the oracular theory, they have few inhibitions about co-operating with members of other disciplines. Today psycholegal research and impact studies also deal with aspects of judicial decision making.[20] The Legal Realists helped to clear the way for this research.

2.1.3 Away with Legal Certainty

Even now the conclusion that legal certainty is an impossibility may still be difficult to accept. But let us face it: legal certainty in the sense that one can tell in advance with a hundred percent certainty how the courts will decide a case, is inconceivable.[21] Such a statement would be a prediction. A prediction is a statement about future events. Propositions of that kind can be neither true nor false. They can only be more or less probable. Instead of hoping that the day will come when legal certainty will reign, it is better to realize that the only concept we can sensibly discuss is that of *legal probability*. Our attention should be devoted to the *degree* of probability one can ascertain, not whether this is, or is not, legal certainty. Before the components that constitute the degree of probability will be identified, some words must be said about the concept of probability.

Expositions of a theory of probability tend to be very technical.[22] None of the chief types of interpretation of probability now in favour can be accepted as wholly satisfactory.[23] For present purposes we may abide by the common-sense view and leave aside the mathematical or statistical theory of probability. 'Probability' implies 'possibility' and excludes 'certainty': what is probable is neither certain nor impossible. Probability is predicated of an event according to a degree to which one rationally can believe that something will occur. When, in ordinary life, it is argued that something will happen, a close examination of the assumptions behind such reasoning reveals the essential role played by previous experience. Built in is the conception that like consequences must ensue from like conditions. There is much truth in the commonly accepted dictum that probability is always relative to evidence. Any probability assertion harks back to assumed enabling conditions.

> If there are *n* mutually exclusive alternatives of the same form, backed by symmetrical reasons, then the *n* probabilities are to be taken as equal.

> From this there follows at once the definition of measure of probability...[24]

Indeed, all that counts is the measure of probability. In the following it will be argued that this measure depends on the success of the analysis of a case and of the frame of mind of the court's members. The term legal certainty may continue to be used, since it is a term familiar to the legal ear. That ear has the tendency to be hard of hearing to anything new. But it should be borne in mind that all that matters is the degree of probability, not certainty. Incidentally, Jerome Frank argues that the calling for legal certainty reveals a desire which he likens to the infant's craving for infallible authority – known as a 'father-complex.'[25]

2.1.4 Elements of the Judicial Decision-Making Process

2.1.4.1 Attitudes of the Judges

Analysis of the judicial process illuminates how the measure of probability can be learned. Rohde and Spaeth made this point in their book *Supreme Court Decision Making.*[26] They have succeeded in predicting with great success the outcome of court cases. During the 1972-1973 terms, 33 of 34 decisions were accurately predicted.[27] This is 97.1%! Rohde and Spaeth focused their investigation on three variables, namely, the attitudes of judges regarding three subjects, and limited their research to certain cases. Their achievements were nonetheless impressive. They gave clues for tackling the problem of legal probability. In the above work an attempt was made to sketch the justices' frame of mind. That is a vital aspect in the decision-making process indeed. Rohde and Spaeth tried to trace the judges' behaviour in similar cases in the past. They found that the judges pick and choose among relevant precedents, but in exercising choice among alternative courses of action, each judge is personally consistent.[28] In order to establish the judges' attitude towards some topics, it is helpful to know how they voted in the past. The institutes of the dissenting and concurring opinion are a great help. Unfortunately, Continental courts prefer anonymity in this matter. This policy does not promote legal certainty. The more abundantly they do so, the better it is. Consequently, the judges should be encouraged to give lectures, teach at universities, write articles, and so on.

Another way to detect the attitudes of the judicial decision-making can be provided by modern logic in the service of law. By means of modern legal logic it is possible to analyse a reasoning. This analysis makes clear which premisses lead to the conclusion. Some premisses may be hidden, some are omitted. The determination of which premisses are hidden or omitted sometimes leads to futile and trivial results. When one says that one goes sailing since the weather forecast is fine after a period of bad weather, one delivers an enthymeme. The implied premiss is obvious. Reasoning of this kind is perfectly acceptable in social intercourse. But in controversial cases it may turn out to be worthwhile to bring the implied premisses to light. It may show the bias or prejudices of the court officials. By investigating a series of court decisions in touchy matters, one may even reveal remarkable predilections and presuppositions. In order to avoid any misunderstanding, it should be underscored that all humans have frames of minds that, consciously or unconsciously, influence their judgments. Jerome Frank once declared that the world's affairs could not go on at all without preconceptions, predispositions, prejudgments. If a person were 'obliged to treat every event as an unprecedented crisis presenting a wholly new problem he would go mad'.[29] Psycholegal research may also help to spot subconscious sensitive zones of members of the courts of law.

Upper courts decisions are worked out in groups.[30] There seem to be certain difficulties that typically arise when people work in small groups.[31] *First*, the members of the group have to be organized: rules for concerted action must be formulated and enforced. Each person must understand the task and be willing to do his or her part. Plans must be made to divide the work up in an effective and equitable way. Conflicts of interest must be resolved and 'unco-operative' people brought into line.[32] *Second*, certain problems require new or unusual solutions. Within a group, established factors such as patterns of communication, social norms, and conformity pressures may keep new or unusual solutions from being uncovered. Thus, for example, although a group may have the potential to generate a large number of ideas, fear of negative evaluations by other group members can limit the variety of the ideas offered. Consequently, small group decision-making tends to preserve established lines, whereas explosions of creative new directions may occur. Therefore, the art of timing changes of the court's policy to decide certain legal matters requires insight into the opinions prevailing within the group, as well as knowledge of how majority coalitions will be formed. This insight can be found among experienced and intelligent observers of the court.

2.1.4.2 More Elements

There are three other aspects to the judicial decision-making process besides those coming from the fact that court officials are social beings and as such have certain attitudes. Those aspects are perhaps easier to grasp. The decision-making process operates as a mould framing the current of the judge's thoughts insofar as certain patterns of reasoning are commonly found among legally trained persons in general and members of the judiciary in particular. These intellectual habits influence the judge's approach to a case at bar and eventually the outcome of the case. Spaeth and Rohde give a rough and unfinished enumeration of these types.[33] These can be found in most handbooks on legal method. They are, *inter alia*, the intention of the makers of the constitution, statute, *etc.*; the purpose of rules; the plain meaning; strict construction; legislative history, *per analogiam* and *a contrario* arguments. Commonly used patterns of legal reasoning can be systematically analysed by recourse to principles of legal logic[34] and the principles of rhetoric and argumentation.[35] The patterns of reasoning are also guided by the framework of an existing legal system. The judiciary is in principle bound by the body of expressed law, statues, *etc.* The legal system provides the relevant substantive and procedural law. The character of the procedure can be of paramount importance as Thibaut and Walker made clear in their *Procedural Justice*.[36] The U.S. due-process clause, as interpreted by the American courts, provides an example: no deprivation of *rights* without proper *procedure.* Judicial innnovation takes place in a relatively small number of cases.[37] The bulk of the cases presented to the courts turn the controversy not upon the rule of law, but upon its application to the facts. (This may require a great deal of choice and creativity.[38]) In another and also considerable percentage, the rule of law is certain, and the application alone is doubtful.

> Finally there remains a percentage, not large indeed, and yet not so small as to be negligible , where a decision one way or the other, will count for the future, will advance or retard, sometimes much, sometimes little, the development of the law. These are the cases where the creative element in the judicial process finds its opportunity and power.[39]

Indeed, this minority of cases is the hardest to predict. On the other hand, these cases are usually in controversial areas, where changes are called for and expected. Again, the timing of the judicial innovation is essential.

A third area of uncertainty in the prediction of court cases lies in the skill to analyse the case, to determine the relevant facts and to use the applicable rules of law. The lawyer who attempts to predict judicial behaviour should realize that he himself is an influential factor in the outcome.

> Many legal scholars, Court observers, and even justices have said that oral arguments can determine the outcome of a case. The late Justice John Marshall Harlan said once that oral argument 'may in many cases make the difference between winning and losing, no matter how good the briefs are.'[40]

The ancient Greeks, who were only too aware of the vital role the rhetorician plays, were very careful in their choice of an ambassador to represent their cause.[41] In general, when people try to influence each other by means of words rather than by terror or intimidation, sophists and their rhetorical skill serve useful purposes.[42]

2.1.4.3 Within the Tides

A fourth source of difficulties concerning the prediction of outcomes of court cases is the fact we are living in changing societies. Worn-out sets of values and ethical norms are being replaced by others. It is not always clear by which. Economic, political and social conditions change too. Some sociologists feel that nowadays a significant number of people tend to regard rules that regulate their personal and interpersonal behaviour as not unconditionally binding.[43] Those rules are regarded as setting an example that ought to be adapted to environmental conditions. Here lies an explanation of the fact that some social rules are being replaced by bargaining systems. This tendency causes both freedom and a sense of insecurity and confusion.[44] In these days of unrest, it is hard to forecast the course of society's development. There is a comfort, though, to be found in Cardozo's observation:

> The great tides and currents which engulf the rest of men do not turn aside in their course and pass the judges by.[45]

The judges change together with the society they serve. This change is, alas, not always proportional. But change there is. Moreover, as

> a final comment on the justices and their value system we should note that the justices collectively mirror the value systems of most Americans. (...) Hence, we may properly infer that these (...) individuals share the same values as the overwhelming majority of Americans. They respond neither to alien nor to inscrutable influences. In this sense, the court is a representative body, even though the justices serve for life and are accountable to no one, save their own conscience.[46]

These observations may be extrapolated to other Western countries, although each country has its own system of calling judges to the bench. One may refute the opinion that the courts represent the value-systems of their countries. Indeed their members are not socially representative of their country, but are often selected from the upper-middle class. Besides this background, their legal training gives them an outlook on the problems which are represented before them, that is naturally a legal one. The judges' attitude do not always reflect the value-system of the community. But the judges do their best when they are guided by precepts of impartiality, learning and integrity. They should render fair judgments, that is, objective and impartial. Moreover, 'a judge is deemed to be capable of setting aside preconceptions when the evidence before him warrants the rejection of previously formed opinions.'[47] Broadly speaking, the opinion one has of whether the judicature is successfully upholding these values and reflects the norms of society, depends on one's political dogmas.

Anyway, it is useless to speculate whether this situation will change or how to find judges who fully represent their community. It is unlikely that this will ever be totally the case. The object of this section is not to discuss the merits of the present situation. It is concerned with the ways in which court decisions can be predicted. A prerequisite to this is to describe what the judicial decision-making process is, not to prescribe how it ought to be. The study of the attitudes of the judges brings to light the values for which they stand and acknowledgement of them makes it easier to predict court cases with success. When we accept that the judge, with all his skill, impartiality, objectivity, bias and prejudice, is the decisive factor in the judicial decision-making process[48], the above observation need not cause any alarm. What we have to do is to focus our attention on identifying attitudes. This inference completes the circle: we arrive at this section's starting point.

2.1.4.4 The Quest for Acceptability

The observations made in section 2.1.4.3 may seem to be somewhat vague. Its controlling presupposition is that court decisions are influenced by the prevailing modes of thinking and widely accepted opinions in a nation. Cardozo referred to this as 'the great tides and currents which engulf the rest of men'. But how can one engaged in predicting court cases deal with this Spirit of Time? This question must be dealt with in a pragmatic manner. If a court decision is broadly accepted by the public, it obviously flows with the 'great tides and currents'.[49] The acceptance of court decisions is the object of the so-called impact studies.[50] Acceptance of court decisions can be *measured* through empirical research.[51]

Court decisions must be acceptable to the litigants and other jurists to ensure that the decision fits into the legal system and the community at large. He who is engaged in predicting judicial decisions may presume that these decisions aim at acceptance by the public at large. Judges are not supposed to impose their own preferences, but the law as they honestly think it is.[52] The courts realize that a legal system can only remain manageable and useful if the bulk of legal decisions are habitually and freely obeyed by the majority of the public.[53] The courts like to keep their system intact. The legal system legitimizes their very existence. The court's pursuance of acceptable decisions is rooted in an instinct of self-preservation. When the courts defy this instinct,other branches of government will remind the courts of nature's precepts.

A famous example of this interaction is President Roosevelt, who was annoyed by the repeated blocking of his New Deal programme by the U.S. Supreme Court. Roosevelt threatened to expand the number of justices from nine to fifteen. That would have enabled him to form a majority, since he would select the six new appointees. The court's response was the 'switch in time that saved the nine.'

We may conclude that he who predicts judicial decisions must analyse the attitudes of the judges and, having established these, calculate how the judges strive for acceptable decisions.

2.1.5 Conclusion

Legal certainty is a highly praised value among legal practitioners as well as laymen. In our changing Western societies, the complaint can be heard again that legal certainty is fading away. In this section the concept of legal certainty is analyzed and it is submitted that we cannot properly speak of 'certainty.' Legal certainty is related to propositions about future behaviour of court officials as to how they will decide cases at bench. Such propositions cannot be expressed with certainty, but only with greater or lesser probability. The degree of probability of these predictions depends upon the skill with which the future behaviour of the bench is estimated. An analysis of the judicial decision-making process is offered. After an investigation of the precepts of Legal Realists, who were concerned with the law-making process of the courts, present studies on this topic were taken into consideration. An evaluation of all the tenets and studies above resulted in the conclusion that the judicial process consists of four components.

Personal. The attitudes of the judges give an important clue to the outcome of a court case. These attitudes can be identified.

Incidental. Analysis of the case and knowledge of applicable rules of law limit the number of alternative outcomes.

Institutional. A legal system narrows the decision-making procedure.

Social. The courts strive for acceptable decisions. Acceptance can be measured. (It is itself the authoritative basis of law.)

Again, the judicial decision-making process is not inscrutable to the extent that we must bid farewell to the value of legal certainty, or rather, legal probability.

2.2 EQUALITY, JUSTICE AND FREEDOM

In chapter 1 the role of standards has been discussed. Standards play an important role in judicial decision-making. After a decision has been rendered, the judge's reasoning is open to analysis. Observations on the analysis of judicial decisions will be made in chapter 6. Standards guide the judge when he is plotting a course; they will help him to find a way out of the problem that the two litigants present before him. They are his points of reference. Arguably, there is a variety of standards. But they can be traced down to a couple of basic standards. That is a matter of definition. Here, standards are understood as values[54] whose purpose it is to justify and rationalize the judicial decision. Values are 'the basis of public support for the activities courts perform.'[55] Jurists are traditionally concerned about three basic standards that always permeate the legal systems of Western societies: Equality, justice and freedom. Western democracies have always cherished these standards. But their meaning has been subject to change. Each of the concepts of equality, justice or freedom may have many conceptions, that are incompatible with each other. Nevertheless, all three concepts have such a strong positive connotation that every judge would be embarrassed if one could impute that his judgments were unfair because of not treating equals alike, or because they are unjust, or violating an individual's freedom. When the imputation is true, the judge has but a cold comfort if he can refer to a specific law to justify his action.

In chapter 3 the relationship between the bench and the political branch of government will be discussed. In the rest of the present chapter it will be argued that the effects of political decisions are felt strongly in the legal system and in the standards that are so dear to the judiciary and the public. This will be done by analyzing the concepts of equality, justice and freedom. So much has been written regarding these topics, that there is no need to add a new analysis. Jurists do not use 'equality' in a *descriptive* but in a *prescriptive* way. Equality has always been defined with respect to relevant criteria. In the past, being a slave or being black implied disqualification. Creatures belonging to these categories were not equal under the law. The Universal Declaration of Human Rights and the Treaty of Rome (1950) have formally put an end to that. They state that all men are born free and are equal in dignity and rights. All men may claim equality before the law. They may also claim equality of opportunity. Western nations adopted the Declaration and ratified the Treaty. Yet we can perceive that in many countries – if not all – some people are more equal than others. There can be a defence for that. Dworkin insists, for instance[56], that a citizen's right to equality means two different sorts of rights, namely, the right to *equal treatment* and the right to *treatment as an equal*. This ingenious distinction shields discrimination. All that matters is valid criteria for the distinction. Stanley I. Benn[57] remarked that:

> Equality very rarely means treating everyone alike; usually it means getting rid of one system of distinctions and replacing it with another.

Today, a popular and generally accepted form of distinction is differentiation according to an individual's need.

> The greater the equality of consideration, the greater the differentiation in treatment. If the latter is not called 'inequality in treatment' it is because the word 'inequality' has acquired, in this sort of context, a pejorative force; 'inequalities' have come to mean *indefensible* differences in treatment.[58]

The decision as to what is defensible and what is not is based on moral or political grounds. Popper[59] contends that:

> Equality before the law is not a fact but a political demand based upon a moral decision; and it is quite independent of the theory – which is probably false – that 'all men are born equal'.

The concept of *justice* is defined by Popper in terms of equality.[60]

> I think that most of us, especially those whose general outlook is humanitarian, mean something like this: (*a*) an equal distribution of the burden of citizenship, i.e. of those limitations of freedom which are necessary in social life; (*b*) equal treatment of the citizens before the law, provided, of course, that (*c*) the laws show neither favour nor disfavour towards individual citizens or groups or classes; (*d*) impartiality of the courts of justice; and (*e*) an equal share in the advantages (and not only in the burden) which membership of the state may offer to its citizens.

Consequently, justice and equality are interdependent. We may come to this conclusion also through a different route. 'The notion of justice consists in a certain application of the notion of equality.'[61] When we compare the most current conceptions of justice, they may seem incompatible.[62]

1. To each the same thing.
2. To each according to his merits.
3. To each according to his works.
4. To each according to his needs.
5. To each according to his rank.
6. To each according to his legal entitlement.

From this the conclusion can be drawn that formal or abstract justice is '*a principle of action in accordance with which beings of one and the same essential category must be treated in the same way'*.[63] These essential categories can contain several relevant criteria. In a particular case the application of all criteria can possibly lead to unacceptable results. Therefore, a necessary complement to 'justice' is equity. This is a tendency to avoid an all too rigid application of relevant criteria as required by justice or equality, when that would in fact result in *inequality*.[64] What counts in practice is not a *concept* of justice, but a particular *conception* of justice. A conception of justice is not to be perceived in terms of equality only. That would lead to absurdities. It may even defeat democratic ideals, for equality can be an antinomy to freedom. Justice should be seen in relation to a scope of other values. It is a useful yardstick to determine whether a legal rule or a judicial decision is a good one, whether it is acceptable. But it is not the only yardstick in helping us to make up our minds. The basic values which underly our Western societies cannot be placed in a pyramidical hierarchy. When it comes to our most precious values, we enter, so to speak, a plain where several values are located.[65] It depends on the case at hand which value or combination of values has more relevance than another. Equality is a fundamental aspect of any conception of justice, along with liberty and so on. But in certain circumstances, equality is *not* a part of justice. Then an unequal treatment of subjects is required by some conception of justice (*e.g.* reversed discrimination).

What is just and equal is decided by moral and political criteria, or more accurately, who belongs to which class and would consequently be entitled to the same treatment and benefits enjoyed by all other members of that class, is determined not by legal but by moral and political considerations. It is obvious that the proper administration of equality and justice necessarily curtails the freedom of the individual. There a compromise is required. In a democracy, the majority makes those decisions. 'The heart of the democratic faith is government by the consent of the governed.'[66] In Western democracies the majorities have agreed to outline the limitation of the individual's freedom through the legal system. The constitution and international treaties like the Treaty of Rome (1950) secure the freedom of the individual.

In this book, it is assumed that at the present time the individual's basic rights – or human rights – that lay the foundation for the protection of his freedom, are sufficiently secured. As long as the courts recognize those rights, the individual's freedom is guaranteed. When the judge must render a decision in a case involving these matters, he must be aware of political implications. An illustration in point is the well-known Bakke decision.[67] The University of California had set quotas favouring some minority groups in order to remedy the result of past discrimination against members of the minority groups involved. Bakke said that the refusal to admit him to medical school, although he had scored better in the admission test than others who were admitted for reasons connected with racial preference, was unlawful. The U.S. Supreme Court agreed and protected this individual's rights. The court was aware of the importance to the nation of the outcome of the case. It knew that the whole country was in a state of expectancy. The court delivered a politically *acceptable* judgment. This judgment was not generally applauded, but it was accepted. It was also an 'act of judicial statemanship'.[68]

CHAPTER 3. A QUESTION OF CONCERN

3.1 THE BENCH AT THE BAR OF POLITICS

Judges hold political[1] opinions like every other member of society. When they are on the bench, they are supposed to neutralize their political convictions and preferences, since they must apply the law in an objective and impartial manner. In chapter 2.1 it was argued that judges are not always successful in suppressing their political sympathies and antipathies. He who wishes to predict court decisions should try to identify the attitudes of the judges and that is all there is to it. In chapter 7.3 methods will be suggested to analyze the reasoning of the court and scrutinize whether there are hidden premisses. In this section, no further attention will be paid to the relationship between judges and politics, a relationship that is the natural consequence of judges being members of society. Nor will attention be paid to judicial selection. It is taken for granted that all judges make decisions according to their preconceived ideas. The system of calling judges to the bench should ensure that the judiciary consists of men and women who are in touch with contemporary conditions. In the following appraisal, the non-personal, institutional relation between the judiciary and the political system of government will be looked at. The relation between the judiciary and politics is a delicate one. This is due to conflicting appeals to the judges. On the one hand, they must remain aloof from politics; on the other, they must participate in them.

Roughly, there are two viewpoints regarding the relation between the bench and politics. The *first* usually prevails in times of social stability when there is a holistic cultural pattern permeating all aspects of society. It is the idea of judges mechanically applying fixed legal rules. Judges 'find' the law, they do not make it, according to this doctrine. Law and politics are separated and so are the judiciary and politics. The *second* doctrine conceives a judge as a politician, who makes political decisions all the time.

Today few judges or lawyers, if any, would accept either of these extreme viewpoints as realistic. Usually the following interaction of courts and politics is recognized:

A. Covert Interaction

1. The courts are a necessary instrument for the implementation of legal rules. Legal rules are reflections of political decisions made by the law-giver. By applying these rules the courts support a political framework. (This standpoint will be illustrated in section 3.3.)

2. The courts are guided by lofty values, like the concepts of equality, justice, equity and freedom. These concepts have conceptions that are politically defined. (This standpoint was worked out in section 2.2.)

3. The impact of judicial decisions may have political consequences. (*E.g.* a preliminary injunction against picketing.)

4. The judge may have a case before him in which the issue is a matter of political controversy. This situation is a variation of the above-mentioned. (*E.g.* impeachments.)

B. Open Interaction

In a democracy, the courts have a special task. They serve as guardians of the rights of the individual. There is no such thing as a self-implementing right and the courts remain inactive until a case is presented to the bench. But once the courts are involved in a case where an individual's basic rights are infringed, they must speak and act with all the power at their disposal. The judges may have to manoeuvre as if they were statesmen. The U.S. Supreme Court did so very skilfully in the segregation cases.[2] It forced the political institutions to make decisions of their own, instead of waiting idly for problem-solving by the Court. The courts should be in the position to defend the individual's basic rights. At present

Western courts are in this position, but they must be alert to remain there. This topic will be expanded in section 3.2.

C. Political Control

When courts have the powerful tool of judicial review they are able to resist legislation they do not like. If courts did not assume that right, either out of ignorance or because the constitution expressly prohibits this, they would be less able to resist pressure from new legislation. In either case, the political branch has final influence through the selection of new appointees. This became clear in a dramatic way in South Africa. The Supreme Court under Justice Schreiner showed hostility toward anti-subversion legislation. The public hysteria against subversive elements was not of a transient character. New appointees to the court were co-operative with the administration and in the end the old judges were in the minority. There is no remedy against the ultimate say of the elected legislator. But the possibilities of the court to resist assaults on the individual's rights can be enhanced. Although the courts have to yield in the end, that moment of surrender can be delayed. A means to reinforce EEC judges will be discussed in chapter 3.2. It may be sad to realize that the courts can only delay the caving in of the individual's rights. It is a comfort, though, that in the past the courts have made clear that a threat against the court itself is resisted strongly. They have done so in various ways.[3] There are no dissenting opinions, then.[4] Judges dislike being told what to do or not to do.

3.2 PRESERVATION OF THE JUDICIARY IN THE EEC

3.2.1 Introduction

In Western democracies, the parliaments are generally expected to act exclusively as legislators. But at present a lawgiving task is thrust upon the courts, whose members are appointed for life and are not responsible to the public in the way elected members of parliament are (*cf.* paragraph 4). Such a tendency seems incompatible with the principle of democracy. It is not likely that the legislature will become the sole legislator again. In this article it is argued that the above tendency does not violate the principle of democracy. On the contrary, it enables the courts to enforce the basic rights of the individuals, a task that is certainly required in the concept of democracy. In addition, suggestions will be made to show how courts can be given the means to carry out that task. But first of all the concept of democracy will be dealt with briefly, 'for I have no desire to speak at length among those who know.'[5]

3.2.2 In Praise of Democracy

> Democracy has seemed the best, the most natural or the inevitable form of government to surprisingly few philosophers. Among these few is Spinoza.[6]

But Spinoza's conviction is not merely a product of abstract reasoning. It displays also his appreciation of the tolerant 17th century Dutch republic.[7] The core of the principle of democracy has been inimitably rendered by Pericles in his funeral oration.[8]

> We live under a form of government which does not emulate the institutions of our neighbours; on the contrary, we are ourselves a model which some follow, rather than the imitators of other peoples. It is true that our government is called a democracy, because its administration is in the hands, not of the few, but of the many; yet while as regards the law all men are on an equality for the settlement of their private disputes, as regards the value set on them it is as each man is in any way distinguished that he is preferred to public honours, not because he belongs to a particular class, but because of personal merits; nor, again, on the ground of poverty is a man barred from a public career by obscurity of rank if he but has it in him to do the state a service. And not only in our public life are we liberal, but also as regards our freedom from suspicion of one another in the pursuits of everyday life; for we do not feel resentment at our neighbour if he does as he likes, nor yet do we put on sour looks which, though harmless, are painful to behold. But while we thus avoid giving offence in our private intercourse, in our public life we are restrained from lawlessness chiefly through reverent fear, for we render obedience to those in authority and to the laws, and especially to those laws which are ordained for the succour of the oppressed and those which, though unwritten, bring upon the transgressor a disgrace which all men recognize.

Up to the present time, this *credo* has scarcely undergone any change. Popper, however, has sensitively refined it for modern needs:

> What I demand from the state is protection; not only for myself, but for the others too. I demand protection for my own freedom and for the other people's. I do not wish to live at the mercy of anybody who has the larger fists or the bigger guns. In other words, I wish to be protected against aggression from other men. I want the difference between aggression and defence to be recognized, and defence to be supported by the organized power of the state.[9]
> It should be mentioned that, from the protectionist point of view, the existing democratic states, though far from perfect, represent a very considerable achievement in social engineering of the right kind. Many forms of crime, of attack on the rights of human individuals by other individuals, have been practically suppressed or very considerably reduced and courts of law administer justice fairly successfully in difficult conflicts of interest.[10]

The principle of a democratic policy is in the words of Popper: 'the proposal to create, develop and protect political institutions for the avoidance of tyranny.'[11]. And he adds:

> How can we so organize political institutions that bad or incompetent rulers can be prevented from doing too much damage?[12]

As a justification for checks and balances to control the rulers,

> the individualist must maintain that the morality of the states (if there is any such thing) tends to be considerably lower than that of the average citizen, so that it is much more desirable that the morality of the state should be controlled by the citizens than the opposite.[13]

We may assume that, at present, a democracy is the most acceptable and appropriate form of government in the EEC countries. But many people question whether it is suited for the future. A forecast of Europe's economic and social evolution tells us that European society of the nineteen-eighties and -nineties is likely to face acute problems.[14] Once more the words of Pericles are recalled:

> ...although only a few may originate a policy, we are all able to judge it.[15]

This may serve as a justification for the controlling presupposition of this section that a democracy is the most desirable form of government for Western countries. No one has all the right answers for future problems in stock. The idea of democracy is that problems are solved by using conviction or perhaps persuasion as the instruments for attaining the best solution. It presumes a dialogue between officials and citizens and implies an appeal to reason and common-sense. A democracy is the most mature way of facing the future.

3.2.3 Problematic Prospects

Futurology is deservedly looked upon with reservation. But from present situations it is possible to extrapolate future trends, the validity of which, however, remains suppositional. It is probable, as Hall[16] points out, that the following six broad trends will pose acute problems for European society during the next two decades.

First, a deepening international economic crisis is imminent. The European economy has been developed to a high degree on the basis of mass-produced industrial goods, that not only circulate in Europe, but also have to provide payments which are needed for imports of vital food and raw materials. Increasingly, the production of these goods has come under the control of multinational corporations. European competitive power is being threatened. On the one hand, as the oil boycott of 1973 shows, European producers are dangerously dependent on imported raw materials from countries that may decide to develop their own manufacturing outlets. At the same time, young industrial workers in Europe and North America are becoming growingly disenchanted with the kind of work assembly-line production offers. Thus the advanced industrial nations are finding it increasingly difficult to compete with their new competitors. For them, it seems, the post-industrial age is truly arriving. But the question remains: how do they now make a living?

Secondly, there is a problem area of world conflict concerning resource use. Limited wars and guerilla activities in areas that contain critical concentrations of industrial vital raw materials will put pressure on Europe also.

The *third* trend is the increasing alienation of many people, especially young people, from the whole system. They are no longer willing to sell themselves to an organization machine in order simply to make money to pursue the goals of an acquisitive society. Rather, they are saying that their central objective is to live a satisfying life - which includes satisfying work.

The *fourth* problem is almost the antithesis of the third. It is the decline and even collapse of the older agrarian society of Europe with its stress on the mutual aid which members of the same extended family provided for each other, and on the security and trust that were only feasible through the face-to-face acquaintance of all in a village. This tendency, of course, does not originate from recent date, but is the sequel to a development that is now having far-reaching repercussions. The result of this collapse is that vital functions, once performed naturally by family members or fellow villagers for each other, now come to be identified as problems to be resolved only through professional bureaucracies. Education and preparation for life become the province of the nursery school, the school system, the college or university plus their supporting bureaucracies. Health becomes the specialized province of doctors, nurses, hospitals and again their supporting bureaucracies. Production of food and other necessities becomes the monopoly of agricultural or manufacturing industries and their supporting distributive networks. Increasingly, stages in the life cycle come to be defined as problems, each requiring a professional bureaucracy to cope with it. Family as a nuclear family seems to dissolve as its members can find more of their satisfaction outside the home. Old people are isolated in senior citizens' colonies or institutions, young people in campus towns. As women assert their right to liberation, career and family maintenance come even more into conflict.

Related to these problems is the *fifth* trend: that of access to information. There is a widespread dissatisfaction with the traditional structure of education. At the same time, the quantity of information received by the ordinary citizen appears almost out of control; but he has little chance of regulating it or using it to his own advantage. The control of information and especially relevant quality of information is not in his hands.

The *sixth* trend is the increasing threat of polarization of our entire society. The immigrant workers, unemployed school leavers, the low-skill workers who cannot find jobs, the old, and all who fall out of the mainstream of society - may let their discontent erupt from time to time in demonstrations, revolts, occupations and general petty disorder.

If these suppositions about future trends come true, they will cause economic change and social unrest. The latter, in turn, may cause severe strain and problems for many citizens. We are inclined to regard problems of the past as less overwhelming than those of tomorrow. Nevertheless, it is worthwhile to look once more at the Athenean society of 400 B.C. The problems at stake there contain elements of present issues. Plato for instance, was worried about the anxious state of mind his fellow citizens were living in. His remedy still appeals to a lot of people in this century: a totalitarian state.[17] There is a danger inherent in the above six trends that governments will feel forced or even obliged to take measures that will jeopardize our democracies. The strength of the resistance against such reactions of both the officials and the citizens fundamentally hinges upon their faith in democracy. At present the EEC countries are democracies. A vital part of democracy is a strong and independent judiciary. In the following it is suggested that the judiciary should be made stronger as a safeguard against possible future assaults on democracy. An outline of the possibilities of the courts in this matter is given in the following paragraph.

3.2.4 The Role of the Courts

In the first paragraph of this section it was observed that the courts have had a *lawgiving task* thrust upon them. This term needs some clarification. The lawgiver gives general rules for the future, based on experience from the past. The judge gives a rule for the past, for facts and actions that have taken place. The administration does both. If there is no applicable rule for a case at bar or if there are conflicting legal rules, then a judge may give a decision that has an implication for the future as well. Even if there is no *stare decisis*, a judicial decision may have persuasive force. When the lawgiver who does not make laws, and the courts are asked to decide cases where no clear rule is available this forces the court to make decisions that obviously have a general meaning for the future. The judge already has the task of making decisions and thus to define the legal concepts of the law. If the law is clear, and if the result is acceptable, the judge has no difficulty in deciding the case. (This observation is made from a legal theorist's point of view. The disentangling of the relevant facts may be difficult.) In the majority of the cases at bench, the judge does not make new law. He merely adheres to a well-established way of interpreting existing law. He may refine the law or re-interpret it in a slightly new way. Or his decision is the first since the law came into existence and he thus becomes the 'trendsetter.' But sometimes a court decision has the effect as if it were an act of parliament. (The former Dutch Chief Justice Wiarda insists in the Netherlands that the lawgiver encourages lawgiving activities of the court by issuing laws that need to be worked out by the court.)[18]

The above lawgiving aspects of the judiciary enable the courts to regulate legal life smoothly and establish a positive public perception of the courts. This presumed task of the courts helps to promote the idea that the courts serve both the public interest and that of individuals. The courts also do so through the impartial weighing of contesting claims of individuals[19] and the protection of the individual against the state.[20] The individual must be alert and take action himself to the court. There is no such thing as a self-implementing right.[21] But most courts are handicapped by insufficient personnel with which to meet a growing and more complex business. Delay in any court results in injustice. Only by speeding up the process of the law and thereby reducing costs, can we eradicate the growing impression that the courts are chiefly a haven for the well-to-do.[22] The courts need suitable quarters, adequate libraries and subordinate court officers. The courts are supposed to render decisions in all areas of the law. But it does happen that, when two lawyers who are experts in a certain field, are presenting the two sides of a case at bar, the bench cannot disguise its perplexity at what those lawyers are talking about. That happens, for example, in cases of competition law, intellectual property or in European law cases.

The power and the impact of a court order depend on the craftmanship and knowledge by which a skilled judge is able to come to a fair, that is, objective and impartial decision. The courts need a legal staff to save time-consuming activities that help forward the judicial decision-making activities and improve their quality. If the courts were in the position to appoint law school graduates as law clerks, they could, for instance, easily find the time to serve as guardians of civil rights. The confidence in the courts as a body to enforce justice would greatly increase if complaints about police behaviour could be submitted to the court by citizens directly and without too many formalities. It is obviously a waste of time and energy to let a judge listen to all those complaints. His law clerks could provide the first aid. They could outline a problem, make the necessary enquiries and present the case to him. The courts also need professionals with non-legal qualifications as advisers and their own experts in accountancy or business administration and should have easy access to the results of sociological investigations on criminal behaviour etc.

The lawgiver sometimes fails in vital areas to issue the laws that are necessary. The judges feel obliged, then, not to sit back and blame the impotent lawgiver but try to solve the case at bar in the most acceptable manner. The court – the supreme court for that matter – could easily improve its service to the public and thus act where the lawgiver fails, if it were allowed to issue *arrêts de règlement*.[23] But the granting of competence to the supreme court to issue *arrêts de règlement* has an unpleasant side effect. The supreme court would usurp the legislative task of parliament. It turns parliament into a mere debating club. Although the boundaries of the activities of the lawgiver and the judiciary are more blurred than the *Trias Politica* doctrine holds, it would do no good to ignore the difference completely. Even a parliament that does not function in a satisfactory way, should not be stripped of its powers. That would jeopardize democracy even more than an imperfectly operating parliament. There are subtle ways for a supreme court to indicate its policy even when a case is not at bench. The members of the supreme court should be active - give lectures, publish articles, teach at law schools, *etc.* Through these activities they can publicly announce a (new) policy of the court. These activities are already taking place, but could still be increased and, perhaps, framed according to plan. Thus the judges, in fact, create *quasi arrêts de règlement*, that are not legally binding, but may turn out to have the same effect. To summarize, the courts must be equipped with all the means to operate actively as enforcers of justice and defenders of the individual. The question arises whether judicial activism is consistent with the democratic organization of our society and whether it fits into our present legal systems.

3.2.5 Judicial Activism

The cleavage between the judiciary on one side and the legislature and the administration on the other, fits into the idea that neither should have the ultimate power. It is sometimes argued that judicial activism implies trespassing on the prerogatives of the administration and parliament. The American legal philosopher Ronald M. Dworkin has argued that judicial activism fits into the constitutional theory on which the Western democracies rest.[24] Dworkin points out that the constitutional provisions that recognize and protect the individual's rights, are framed in a specific manner. They are abstract or 'vague' in the sense that they do not contain specific and limited rules. They leave room for reasonable men of good will to disagree. Their meaning develops and alters as a natural consequence of the passing of time.

Dworkin explains this by means of a theory of meaning. He maintains that the constitutional provisions contain *concepts* and not *conceptions*. According to Dworkin a conception is a proposition for a specific case. A concept is a frame in which the numerous conceptions may fit. A concept can be an appeal to morality. A conception is a spatio-temporal solution that comes, prevails and is abandoned in history. After Dworkin has put the matter in this light, he discusses the programmes of *judicial activism* and of *judicial restraint*.[25] According to the latter,

> courts should allow the decision of other branches of government to stand, even when they offend the judges' own sense of the principles required by the broad constitutional doctrines, except when these decisions are so offensive to political morality that they would violate the provisions of any plausible interpretation, or, perhaps, when a contrary decision is required by clear precedent.[26]

The programme of judicial activism holds that courts should accept the constitutional provisions in the sense of *concepts* that need interpretation before they can be applied to the case at bar. Dworkin finishes his defence of judicial activism by demolishing every argument that insists that judicial restraint fits better into a democratic constitutional theory.[27] He says that if we take a democracy as a system that grants rights to individuals against the majority, it is fairer and sounder to abstain from judicial deference. The majority (the state) should not decide what specific rights the individual possesses. The courts are trained to give fair judgments, that is, objective and impartial. The courts are trained also to weigh competing claims and diverging interests.

It may be concluded that both the recognition of a lawgiving judicial activity and a policy of judicial activism fit into western legal systems. They are compatible with the principle of democracy, but this conclusion should not be accepted without the following consideration. Judicial activism can be used to *violate* basic rights as well. Indeed, it is a progressive method that can be misused by conservative courts. In the nineteen-thirties Roosevelt's New Deal was blocked by a conservative Supreme Court. At that time progressive lawyers favoured a policy of judicial restraint. The history of the Weimar republic provides other examples.

Today a progressive lawyer such as Dworkin promotes the idea of judicial activism. But there is a danger lurking in judicial activism. An independent court can frustrate a law by giving unorthodox interpretations of it. Of course, the lawgiver should take into consideration the tendency of the courts to decide certain legal matters. The lawgiver should take care that a law is acceptable not only to the voters who must elect a new parliament, but to the judiciary as well. Regardless of his political preferences, judicial activism is a good thing provided the judge is a good judge. If he is not very competent or his integrity doubtful, one cannot but wish an active lawgiver who leaves little room for the judge's frivolities. In most Western countries, attention is paid to the education and training of judges. That seems indeed the best policy. The quality of the officials is the ultimate warrant of a legal system that has to ensure that justice is done. Therefore, we should focus our attention on the assistance the judge could use to ensure he can meet his responsibilities.

3.2.6 More Help to Brothers in Law

Again, the possibilities of the courts to act as guardians of basic rights can be improved by supplying extra legal and non-legal staff. The business of the courts is continually increasing in volume, importance and complexity. Further improvement should be reached by changing the kind of cases that can be presented to the court. It is a waste of time, for example, to let the courts adjudicate divorce cases. The majority of such cases could easily be handled by the administration. The right to appeal should remain for those who disagree with the decision of the administration concerning the only two issues in a divorce that should be of concern to the law: money and decisions concerning the children. The courts should be enabled to devote time to cases that do matter for the average citizen's confidence in the law, such as public order (including the efficacy of police behaviour, assault and battery, mob hooliganism, etc.). Public confidence in civil law will be boosted when it is possible to obtain a quick and inexpensive decision regarding small claims.

All this holds as long as our present legal and political systems do not change. It has been argued in this article that the courts are bulwarks in the defence of basic rights and that their position should be reinforced. But what will be the case when the political systems in one or more EEC countries change to the point that they become a threat to the individual's basic rights? Such a change is not impossible. The historian Walter Laqueur[28] observes, for example, that terrorism creates much public consternation. Once insecurity spreads and terror becomes a real danger, the authorities are no longer blamed for disregarding basic rights in their struggle against terrorists. On the contrary, the cry goes up for more repressive measures, irrespective of the price that has to be paid in basic rights. An elected government and an elected parliament, that must control the government, may yield to the assault on basic rights. The judge is the only authority left to serve, dispassionately, as a guardian of the individual's basic rights. This counts very much since terrorists are hardly a real danger for society. Laqueur insists that while they are a nuisance for the public, kill innocent people, and may cause immeasurable grief and sorrow, they are politically weak. Terrorism will continue to cause destruction and the loss of human life. It will always attract publicity, but, politically it tends to be ineffective. It may only have the side effect that it encourages attacks on basic rights. If a political system through whatever cause takes a wrong turning, a solution must be found, first of all, at a political level. If that fails, the courts eventually are helpless and defenceless. If the fundamental principles of individual freedom yield to usurpation by the administration or the military, a judge can only seek consolation in Chief Justice Taney's words as pronounced in 1861[29] in full expectation that he, too, would be imprisoned:

> In such a case, my duty was too plain to be mistaken. I have exercised all the power which the constitution and laws confer upon me, but that power has been resisted by a force too strong for me to overcome.

Judges are appointed for life. Although they are independent, no judge would maintain that he is fully free from the administration. Nor is he free from social control from his colleagues. The administration has a say in the appointment of a judge, his promotion, his transfer to more agreeable courts, in short, his career. The judge is not able to select the kind of work he wishes to do. All courts have their internal planning schemes, decreeing which judge shall do criminal law, intellectual property, bankruptcy, family law, etc. The judge will become even more dependent on the administration when he has the staff he is entitled to. The judge is vulnerable to harassment and pressure. If a government in an EEC country goes awry, it has the means to influence the court. The judge could use support in this matter.

3.2.7 Some Suggestions

When a judge fails to receive help from his own country when seeking to act as a defender of basic rights, he may feel a need to obtain it from outside. But that implies a violation of sovereignty. Any plea that foreigners should be entitled to interfere in a Member State's system of justice should be regarded with reserve. At the present time, however, part of their national sovereignty has been abandoned by the Member States of the EEC. There is, for instance, the Court of Justice, whose duty it is to see that the EEC Treaty is properly enforced. This treaty is an economic treaty, though. But the Court has decided that it is also a part of its task to protect the basic rights of the individual. It has ruled that 'the basic personal rights are contained in the general principles of Community law, whose observance the Court of Justice must ensure'.[30] And also: 'The protection guaranteed by fundamental rights is, as regards Community law, assured by various provisions in the Treaty, such as articles 7 and 40 (3); this is written law supplemented in its turn by unwritten Community law, derived from the general principles of law in force in Member States.'[31] In the Handelsgesellschaft case the Court has put the same matter in different words: 'the recognition of basic rights is one of the general principles of law which the Court of Justice must safeguard'.[32] The Court continues in this Handelsgesellschaft case: 'In fact, respect for fundamental rights forms an integral part of the general principles of law protected by the Court of Justice. The protection of such rights, whilst inspired by the constitutional traditions common to the Member States, must be ensured within the framework of the structure and objectives of the Community.' The policy of the Court is justified by article 164 of the EEC Treaty: 'The Court of Justice shall ensure that in the interpretation and application of this Treaty the law is observed.' The Court even recognized legal *principles*: 'In accordance with a principle common to the legal system of the Member States, the origins of which may be traced back to Roman law (*sc.* D 1.2.3.26 and 28) when a legislation is amended, unless the legislature expresses a contrary intention, continuity of the legal system must be ensured.'[33]; and also the *non bis in idem* principle[34] and the principle of legal certainty or security.[35] This practice of the Court of Justice is in accordance with the official policy of the community institutions, who stress publicly their concern with basic rights.[36]

Consequently, the EEC Treaty could be amended in such a way that any judge would have a right to appeal to the Court of Justice to obtain an injunction against the harassing administration. Then, an appeal would also be possible against the decision of judges, who put a fellow-judge out of the main stream of cases that come to his court, and against other decisions which make it impossible for a judge to perform his task properly. The right of appeal has a deterrent effect on government activities against a judge. Until now, the Court of Justice has been successful in urging governments and national courts to comply with the EEC Treaty as the Court reads it.[37] The Court has not only an official judgment at its disposal. Its judges have made effective use of their standing in private conversations too. The efficacy of these extra-legal activities became clear when the Italian government (see note 37) did not take adequate measures to comply with the judgment of 10 December 1968 for more than three years. The Court's judges went to Rome and talked the Italian government into submission. At that time, the government could not afford a harsh judgment of the Court: the Italian public opinion is in favour of the EEC and the opposition in parliament would have taken advantage of a condemnation by the Court. The Court's judges skilfully played their hand. The suggestion to amend the EEC Treaty implies that an economic community institution is granted the authority to intrude in a nation's delicate political affairs. But the idea of an absolute sovereignty of Member States has already been abandoned with the introduction of the EEC Treaty. The suggestion to remedy political problems by means of an economic EEC Treaty and an economic court is not very elegant from a theoretical point of view. But it is a solution that can be incorporated relatively easily into the present legal system of the Common Market. Other possibilities seem to be too far reaching, such as a special High Commission on the Judiciary of the EEC, elected by judges of the Member States. Another possibility is to incorporate the assistance of the Court of Justice in the set of special rules for the protection of basic rights within the Community, that the European Parliament proposes.[38] The insertion of the Court of Justice as argued in this section in the protection of the judiciary is perhaps the solution that fits best in the already available legal framework of the legal systems of the EEC countries. This consideration is inspired by the fact that the EEC countries give evidence of their unwillingness to sacrifice their political independence. They will be reluctant to give up their sovereignty regarding their judiciary, an independent judiciary being a vital aspect of political independence. The EEC Treaty with its overriding impact on legal life in the EEC, and, in particular, the Court of Justice, are both precedents, so far as curtailment of the power of the judiciary is concerned.[39] Since the idea of the national sovereignty of the judiciary is a delicate one, the initiative to interfere could better come from a national judge than from a community institution.

Not only a government may go awry but a judge may also deviate from integrity. In this article, it has been taken for granted that we now have a sound and reliable judiciary. Hence, an irresponsible judge is merely an exception. The various national legal systems of the EEC countries provide means for removing such judges and quashing their decisions.

3.2.8 Conclusion

If we take the uncertain future of Europe's economic and social development seriously, we may conclude that a strain will be inevitable on the legal systems of the EEC countries insofar as they contain safeguards for the protection of the individual's basic rights. The courts are the warrant that these rights are enforced and their task is likely to become increasingly difficult. They could be supplied with the means to meet future demands. Several suggestions have been made. A *legal staff* enables the judge to render a decision that is acceptable, because of its legal qualities, its social implication and its doing justice to the issue which the parties involved have raised. *The recognition of the legislative role* of the courts should go together with the acceptance of the authority to issue *quasi arrêts de règlements*. The acknowledgement that *judicial activism* fits into our present legal system and is consistent with the principle of democracy would help to straighten our democracies. A rider to the EEC Treaty to the effect that any judge could *appeal to the Court of Justice* to obtain injunctions against any harassment by the administration would also be a valuable innovation.

CHAPTER 4. A DIFFERENT VIEWPOINT

4.1 AN INVENTORY OF THE JUDGE'S EQUIPMENT

In section 3.2, it has been argued that the judiciary needs more defence systems. But it is uncertain whether the necessary elements will be provided by the legislator. Even a relatively simple provision like the proposed rider to the EEC Treaty will meet much resistance. However, this and the other requests for improvement of the judicial performance are modest. They are matters of finance and not really matters of principle. In section 3.2, it was argued that a 'clear and present danger' is the creeping influence of the administration. This influence will increase when the courts receive the required aid of professional management and get access to some non-legal disciplines. It is obvious that the courts need insulation against looming dependancy. But enough has been said about this in the previous chapter.

The judges of the Common Market could learn from their American brethren, not only about the use of law-clerks to assist with research and the staff of expert economists, sociologists and penologists to advise on the decisions to be made, but also about the *Brandeis* brief and the *amicus curiae* brief.

When Louis Brandeis was not yet a justice at the U.S. Supreme Court, but a lawyer, he submitted in a case a brief which contained only a couple of pages relating to the law, but many pages describing how other countries resolve the issue in question, the consequences of deciding the case for the plaintiff or the defendant and the opinions of economists and other experts. In some European legal systems, for example, the Dutch system, counsel may submit a brief of this kind to the court, if he pleases. In others, for example, the English[1], this would not be accepted. There, the arguments of counsel concentrate on the point that his client has legal rights which the courts should enforce. This narrowing of the problem to only the legal aspects of the case, is due to the fact that the English courts will listen to little else.[2]

The *amicus curiae* brief enables groups, which are not parties to the action, but are vitally concerned with the outcome of the court case, since they will be affected by it, to submit evidence to the court. This brief is based on the assumption that judicial decisions formally bind only the litigants (who may be numerous in a 'class action'), but may have a much wider impact. The admission of the *amicus curiae* brief is in fact an acknowledgement of the legislative role of the courts. Both briefs make it easier for the courts to use law as an instrument of social change. Political questions can be made into legal ones. The assumed social responsibility of the courts may promote a gradual and harmonious development of society. Thus, the courts are able to co-operate with politicians, union leaders and social reformers.[3]

The judiciary in other countries than the U.S. need not wait for the legislature to grant permission for the acceptability of these briefs. The courts can simply assume their admissibility. There would be no one to challenge that policy. European courts need not remain passive until the legislator gives them new tools to facilitate more efficient participation in piecemeal social engineering. The judiciary needs a fresh look at the instruments they now have at their disposal. A new application of an available instrument makes in fact a new instrument. This proposition needs clarification, which can be achieved by analyzing an aspect of a legal system the author is most familiar with, that is, the Dutch system. For readers who are only interested in the point that will be made, a summary follows in chapter 4.2. They may disregard chapter 4.3.

First, certain measures that would be required from the legislature to reduce the burden of the judges' caseloads.[4]

a. More judges.
b. Less law. The legislature produces complex situations by issuing a multitude of laws without paying much attention

to the practical consequences of that output or taking into consideration the consistency and workability of the legal system. It is no exception that contradictory laws are sometimes issued.

c. Diminish the issues that can be brought before the court. There is no need, for example, in the Netherlands, to bother the courts with all the divorces. The administration is able to get people married. It should also be able to get them divorced. Appeal to the courts should be possible when there remains disagreement relating to the children or to financial matters. Every country has examples of problems which are presented to the bench, but which could better be solved by other means, thus relieving the caseload of the court.

d. Court reorganization. The notorious Italian *Valpreda* case is a recent example of uncertainty as to the competence of the court preventing due process in a reasonable amount of time. Sometimes civil and criminal procedure prevail over the substance of law.

e. Eliminate juries. They are an anachronism.[5] This recommendation may sound shocking to the English and Americans. For civil law countries without juries this proposal would be less so. Perhaps it may deserve consideration to limit the range of cases in which trial by jury is possible.

f. Speedy trial laws. Recent studies, for example, in the Netherlands[6], may justify the conclusion that lawyers and not the courts are the main obstacles against prompt proceedings.

This list of solutions that needs handling by the legislature, could be made more elaborate. The above examples are merely the most obvious items to be worked out. In the next chapter, a summary is given of section 4.3. There it will be argued that the judge is quite able to help himself. If he interprets existing legal rules differently, he may achieve remarkable results in making the legal system operate more efficiently.

In the Netherlands, keen publishers discovered a huge market for scandalous magazines that mainly contain gossip regarding filmstars, TV personalities, sportsmen, public figures, public officials, members of the royal family, *etc.* Many readers are pleased with a newly published magazine. The Netherlands has a population of 14 million. The gossip magazines reach an estimated 5 million readers. Many libelled personalities are not amused. Means of protection of the libelled seem to be inadequate. Dutch courts have not the habit of awarding large sums for damages. Litigation is expensive and takes a lot of time: a year or more. There is a growing demand for new legislation that will restrain abuse of the freedom of the press by gossip publications. But a serious threat is involved in curtailing the freedom of speech, even when that curtailment only aims at gossip. In section 4.3 it will be argued that new legislation is not necessary to deal with this unwanted development in popular publications.

Dutch civil procedure authorizes the Presidents of the 16 district courts to hear cases in summary proceedings. A prerequisite is that there is a matter of great urgency, requiring a court order at once. In addition, the President may order the defendant only to do or to forbear some act. The President's injunction is preliminary in the sense that the litigants are supposed to use the injunction as a cooling off of the conflict. The civil procedure system assumes that the litigants go to court and have their case tried in the regular way. The court's decision is final, if not appealed upon. The President's judgment may not prejudice the ensuing judgment of the court.

During the last two decades, the Presidents of the district courts were increasingly asked to give judgment. There are various reasons for this development. Summary proceedings go fast, are quite informal, are cheaper than ordinary litigations, while the standing and skill of the Presidents generally warrant sound decision-making and acceptable decisions. At present, the Presidents tend to ignore the defence that the case is not a matter of great urgency. Statistics show that appeals are exceptions to the rule that the parties accept the President's decision as final. Summary proceedings are unfit for certain areas of the law. But they apply to libel cases. The Presidents are increasingly being asked to order the rectification of libels. To their dismay, libelled personalities discover that an occasional injunction to rectify does not discourage the gossip industry. Today there is an increasing demand for legislative remedies curtailing the excesses of the free press. In section 4.3, it is contended that there is no need for such an *ultimum remedium* that sets precedents and may have disagreeable side-effects. There is no objection to be found in civil procedure against the President's order to the defendant to pay damages for libel. Technically speaking, such a payment would be an advance of damages. If the President did so and if payment for damages were substantial, libelled persons would have an ideal remedy. In this way, the call for legislative intervention curtailing free speech becomes obsolete. Thus, merely by looking at his juridical tools in a new way, the judge is able to prevent an attack on the individual's rights to free speech, while protecting the individual's right to privacy.

4.3 A PLEA FOR THE PRESIDENT

4.3.1 Growing Gossip

As in other countries in recent years, the Netherlands have been subjected to the impact of a new and more lurid expression of journalistic permissiveness: gossip columns and magazines consisting purely of gossip and scandal-mongering about public figures like singers, filmstars, TV personalities, sportsmen, politicians, members of the royal family, and so on. It is an undisguised form of commercialism. The most infamous Dutch gossip magazines have a sale of 1.3 million copies a week.[7] Circulation is increasing. The publishers and editors are merely dealing in printed paper and know what kind will sell best, thanks to market research data. It seems that many public figures who are featured conspicuously in the gossip magazines do not object to being exposed to the glare of publicity, which will cause their fame, popularity and 'market value' to rocket. The film editor Wim Verstappen contends[8]: 'Many gain from the gossip press'. As a means of obtaining free publicity for movies while they are being shot and during later screening in the cinemas, he thinks that the gossip press is useful. He also contends that the quality press arbitrarily withholds relevant and important information. He points to examples of unusual behaviour in private of important public officials and claims that the sensationalism of the popular press is caused by the failure of the 'decent' press. Verstappen feels that intrusion on their privacy is the price public figures have to pay for their popularity. In addition, many of them are so eager for publicity that one need not feel sorry when they are occasionally treated unfairly. Finally, if the gossip is shameless, the victim must strike back hard.

In a Dutch television programme called *De Wereld van het Nieuws* ('The World of the News'), Prince Claus, former Secretary of State Jaap Boersma, union leader Wim Kok, and others talked about gossip that consisted of malicious inventions and complained of intolerable invasions of their privacy. They found the gossip damaging and harassing and felt a sense of frustration at their powerlessness to counter it. The publisher of *Story*, one of the sensation magazines, had a different opinion. In the programme of 1 March 1979, he said that one could always go to court if there was real damage. He added that his company could afford to pay for damages if the court awarded them. But, he said, parties just do not go to court, since there is no damage. One may not like to be in the public eye. Incidentally, that once happened to him, and the editors and journalists rightfully did not care, he said. The points of view of editors and journalists on the one hand and of public figures on the other differ considerably. The former group assume that news about the private life of well-known personalities is news that is fit to print. The best-known writers of gossip columns who were interviewed made clear that they did not care a straw for the privacy of others. They made a good living while public figures got free publicity and the readers what they paid for. But the consequence is that untrue statements are published about the private life of public figures and public officials who may object.

It is difficult to take action against this. What help does the law offer? To ask for criminal prosecution for libel leads to involvement of the injured party in the criminal procedure, which is most undesirable. According to G.E. Langemeijer, a former Attorney-General at the Dutch Supreme Court, it is one's duty to prevent a friend from trying to make the police and the public prosecutor prosecute the libeller.[9] Disciplinary law for journalists fails to offer adequate protection for the libelled.[10] A litigation before a civil court takes a lot of time, is expensive and gives rise to a new crop of renewed publications in which the defamatory statements are repeated. Another disadvantage is that Dutch courts award very small sums for damages in libel cases.

There is an alternative near at hand, though. The Presidents of the 16 district courts of the Netherlands may hear cases in summary proceedings. These proceedings do not take up much time. They are less expensive than ordinary litigations. Summary proceedings would be an ideal weapon against libel, especially originating from gossip, if only they gave the plaintiff *financial* relief as well. As matters now stand, the latter has to pay his lawyers and is able to obtain an injunction requiring the gossip magazine to publish a rectification and apology. If the defendant does not offer to pay damages, the Presidents of the district courts assume that they do not have the authority to order indemnification. The plaintiff would still have to go to court and start an ordinary litigation for damages. Again, Dutch courts traditionally award small sums.

The plaintiff's defencelessness encourages publishers, editors and journalists in the infamours gossip industry to do as they please. While they make profit by publishing untrue or misleading information, they only face the risk of an injunction to publish a rectification and not to repeat their libel. As they calculate their profits, they naturally pay little heed to possible liability for damages. If this situation were different, no doubt the policy of the editors would alter and, if the editors were reluctant to change their policy, the publisher, who is liable according to the law, would certainly decide on another policy.

A different system of awarding damages would not be enough

relief for libelled persons. They still have to go through lengthy and costly litigation. If the President of the district court would only issue an injunction to publish a rectification *and* to pay substantial damages, the libelled person would have an ideal weapon at his disposal. There would still remain the disadvantage, of course, that summary proceedings renew publicity regarding the libellous statements. But that publicity follows shortly after the publication of the libel itself. That may, in fact, already be a prelude to the rectification. (The President can take into consideration whether the summary proceeding itself is satisfactory to the victim. The latter must be able to show that his reputation is not something to be toyed with.) In the Netherlands, it is generally assumed that, according to the law, the President cannot issue an injunction to pay damages, since it would be incompatible with the nature of a summary proceeding. This proceeding is supposed to result in a court order to do or to forbear doing something, but is not meant to declare the rights of the litigants in a final sense. In the following, this assumption will be treated in detail.

4.3.2 Summary Proceedings and Payment of Damages

In 1946 E.M. Meijers wrote in the preface of his standard work on 'Summary Proceedings'[11]: 'Today one hears voices of those who wish to diminish the summary proceedings, for instance, in labour conflicts as well of those who wish to expand it, for instance, to turn it into a general summary proceeding. Let the summary proceeding remain as it is. No country has granted such a large discretion to the judge in summary proceedings as the Netherlands have. This is a cause for satisfaction and contentment.'

By now the summary proceeding has undergone quite a development. Its character and function have been changed. The number of summary proceedings has grown.[12] This change is obvious, too, when one looks at the President's handling of the statutory requirement of 'great urgency' for a summary proceeding. In an increasing number of cases, the President is willing to admit cases for hearing. A typical example is the attitude of the President of the District Court of

Amsterdam, Mr. W.J. Borgerhoff Mulder[13], who readily overrules the defence's plea that the case before his bench is not a matter of 'great urgency'. This attitude is quite common among presidents throughout the country. Schenk, a former President, observes[14]: 'Because the judgment of the President is of a preliminary nature, he may not render a declaratory (*i.e.* a judicial declaration of some right) judgment.' In a footnote Schenk continues[15]:

> In my opinion, it is a matter of terminology. There is no sound objection to a declaratory judgment, because the President does render through his opinion a decision regarding rights (*cf.* Zonderland, p. 147). Of course, the judgment has legal consequences for the litigants and has an influence upon their legal position, but, according to common terminology, it is incorrect to call it a 'legal decision declaring rights'; as Wijckerheld Bisdom rightly observes in his review of Zonderland's book in R.M. Themis (a legal journal), 1975, p. 85: a declaratory judgment in a summary proceeding is a *judicium non dabile*[16], because it does not prejudice other judgments.[17] This must be made obvious in the wording of the judgment. Therefore, it is commendable to underscore the nature of the judgment if the President, when he discusses the rule of law in his opinion, adds that it is preliminary opinion that this or that is the legal position of the litigants. To incorporate a declaratory statement in his judgment only causes confusion for the layman, to whom the judgment is addressed after all. The judgment should only contain the injunction (or the refusal to grant it).

Schenk renders examples for terminology to be used by the President to give the impression that the injunction is provisional only. According to Schenk, a legal attachment may not be nullified in a summary proceeding. The President must order the withdrawal of the attachment. But if that order is given in a case where the attachment is on a foreign vessel (the attachment causing jurisdiction for the court) and the ship sails then away, the result is exactly the same as if the attachment were nullified.

The fact that a judgment following a summary proceeding may, in fact, be the last word in a particular case, does not bother the President of the District Court of Amsterdam. Borgerhoff Mulder contends[18] that he can only render an injunction to do or to forbear from doing something. But he suggests that it is a matter of the attorney's skill to operate with civil procedure in order to formulate what he wishes in the form of an order to do or to forbear. Even further goes the opinion of Heemskerk[19] who asserts that there are only arguments in favour of the possibility to render a declaratory judgment in a summary proceeding. The term 'injunction' or 'order' is so vague and so general that it may as well cover a declaratory judgment. He adds: Why should we interpret that concept in a narrow way, whereas legal practice requires an extended interpretation? Heemskerk's opinion is interesting, because, in 1976, he argued that if the plaintiff asks in a summary proceeding for a declaratory judgment, the President must give judgment for the defendant.[20] Heemskerk's change is significant for the role of the President and his summary proceeding as it is generally perceived today. Please help me and readjust the scale of interests between the defendant and myself. The President is requested to mould the legal system to ensure that justice is done. As it happens, his judgment is the final word. Litigants do not appeal with great success, if at all.[21] They rarely submit the case to the district court after the President has tried it.

The President as a *iudex unus* plays a very necessary role that is generally applauded. His fast, informal hearings and especially the short term he takes to render his decision are appreciated.[22] The litigant has no desire to await the end of a long litigation. Summary proceedings can be very useful when negotiations have come to a deadlock. Any outcome of a summary proceedings changes the situation for the parties involved and that change alone may be enough to bring a solution within reach. This may sound unlikely or theoretical, but practice proves this proposition to be true. Another cause of the increase in the number of summary proceedings is also the fact that the Presidents are able judges who render judgments of high quality. This improves the impact and the acceptability of these judgments. The flexible rules of civil procedure regarding summary proceedings enable the President to give judgments that go to the heart of the matter and leave aside legal intricacies. This is also a cause for the increasing number of summary proceedings.

As the line of development of summary proceedings stands

now, the President is authorized to order payment of an advance of damages. There are some precedents.[23] He gives judgment for the plaintiff, if one cannot reasonably doubt that the defendant is liable and the scale of interests of the litigants is in favour of the plaintiff. It is not necessary that there is a financial state of emergency. The advance may be as large as the total liability. According to the body of expressed law, the President can order *in integrum restitutio*. He is authorized to issue an injunction to the effect that the consequences of a tort are undone. The President never worries that his injunction is, in fact, causing a final and practically non-reversable situation.[24] By now, the conclusion may safely be drawn that the Dutch legal system is developing to a point where the President may in summary proceedings give judgments which are *in fact* declaratory and contain injunctions that are *in fact* orders to pay damages. This conclusion is not as bizarre as some jurists may think. Present civil procedure comes from the 19th century. It is traditionally interpreted that the President could by no means render declaratory judgments or order payment of damages. But why should we feel bound by a 19th century legislator? R.M. Dworkin has pointed out[25] that clauses in the constitution, acts and statutes are *concepts*. The judge defines a concept in a particular case according to some *conception*. The efficacy of a legal system hinges upon the assumption that a judge must define legal concepts in relation to a particular case at bench. In the 1980s, it is suitable for the President to take into consideration the above development of the summary proceeding and to give judgments that are *in fact* declaratory and contain *in fact* an order to pay damages.

4.3.3 Assessment of Damages

The next question we must deal with is how to assess damages. Public relations consultants are able to give an estimation of costs to boost someone's damaged reputation. The 'marketing value' of well-known public figures can be calculated. If one could ascertain a man's discredit or loss of reputation in the estimation of others, or his exposure to hatred, contempt or ridicule, or the injury of his reputation in his office, trade or profession, or the injury to his financial credit caused by the libel, then the assessment of damages is possible.[26] Not only the stature and standing of the victim are relevant, but also the nature of the libel, the mode and extent of publication, the absence of refusal of any retraction or apology, and the whole conduct of the defendant from the time when the libel was published down to the very moment of the verdict. As a rule of thumb, the President should try to readjust the scale of values, no more and no less. That is, after all, the purpose of a summary proceeding. Although it is a fiction, the President must try to put the plaintiff in a position as if he had never been libelled. Dutch courts have the habit of arguing that money and a man's reputation are an incompatible quantity and quality. They draw the conclusion that one must not try to equate these. Consequently, libelled persons only receive token damages. The President should come to a more sophisticated round of thinking and look perhaps at his Anglo-American brethern to see how skilfully they assess damages. There is no need to be afraid that the award of damages will get out of hand. In the Netherlands, there are no juries to let sentimental feelings prevail over reason. Moreover, lawyers cannot work on a no cure-no pay basis.

If the plaintiff is a man of slender means and has a taste for fast spending, the defendant is put into an unfair position if the President's judgment is reversed on appeal. When such a defence is raised, the President may order the defendant to put the payment into a bank account that will be blocked, unless the defendant fails to appeal within a very short time. There seems to be no remedy if the hearings on appeal generate a new outburst of defamatory comment. But the court of appeal may take this into consideration and assess a higher amount for damages.

The purpose of this chapter is not to suggest that the judiciary should drastically change civil procedure and adopt a general admittance of summary proceedings for all cases. Such a change of policy should be left for the legislature to decide. But there are two sound reasons in favour of the proposed slight change of view by the President to the result that in some cases a maligned person has adequate means to react against malicious imputations. *First*, there is a public outcry against libellous gossip. A considerable part of the public seems to enjoy this development. But nowadays the call for legislation to curb this development is being heard more often and more strongly. Such legislation implies constitutional or statutory abridgment of freedom of speech. Reduction of the constitutional right of freedom of speech is highly undesirable. But when members of parliament perceive positive results in elections thanks to favouring curtailment of a basic right in western societies, they yield to the popular demand. The judiciary can avert this danger by slightly changing its perception of civil procedure.

Secondly, most people have an awareness which the late Edmond Cahn called a 'sense of injustice'.[27] Rather than define what 'justice' is, people experience a 'sense of injustice'. A controlling presupposition of this chapter is that the gossip press is run for profit according to the rules of modern management. Publishers, editors and journalists earn a comfortable living at the expense of innocent and rather defenceless people who stimulate the demand for sordid news just because they happen to be well-known. If the judicatory permits this situation to continue, although it has the means within reach to put a stop to it, it falls short in its task of administering justice. It would fail to fulfil common expectations of society. It would forsake its duty if it permitted injustice to continue. If the judiciary would issue injunctions requiring gossip-mongers to pay a heavy penalty for their infamous behaviour, the profit conscious publishers of gossip magazines and columns would be more disposed to curb the scurrilous activities of their editors and journalists.

4.3.4 Conclusion

The recent increase in libellous gossip has caused concern to a significant number of public figures and public officials as well as a considerable part of the population. It is repeatedly argued that new legislation is wanted to control this increase. It is generally assumed that the present legal system fails to supply adequate relief. Here, it is argued that the judiciary has the means near at hand to make obsolete new legislation curtailing the freedom of the less honourable parts of the press. What is needed is a slightly different outlook by the judge regarding certain rules of civil procedure. Several justifications for this proposed re-examination of available legal instruments are offered. The new outlook is fully acceptable in the Dutch legal system as it stands now. In addition, it is contended that a failure of the judiciary to adopt the proposed policy results in injustice.

4.3.5 Against Judicial Interventionism

A final warning should be added here. Section 4.3 as well as section 3.2.5 contain arguments in favour of judicial activism. But judicial activism must not lead to *judicial interventionism*: an arbitrary exercise of power by the court. It does not matter that a law is unfair as long as it is applied equally to all. The judge must decide what the law is and must try not to give way to his sense of justice, morality or fairness without being able to keep in line with the legal system. He ought to insist on reason in the judicial process, on analytical coherence and on principled judgment.[28] Reason may be used to question old values. If they do not stand the test of critical analysis, the judge is free to look for alternatives. In fact, the restraints of reason tend to ensure his independence and keep him free from the demands that so often enchain other public officials. They make it possible for him to oppose the will and faith of the majority. But the courts must keep in mind that their effectiveness 'depends substantially on confidence, on what is called prestige. It is likely, therefore, (...) that there is a natural quantitative limit to the number of major, principled interventions the court can permit itself....'[29]

CHAPTER 5. DISCRETION

5.1 LEGAL LIMITATIONS TO DISCRETION

Ever since legal rules had to be adjudicated, the topic of discretion has been a controversial issue.[1] 'Discretion' refers to the freedom of the judge to apply the law. There have been roughly two extreme attitudes towards discretion, and many in between. According to adherents of codified legal systems, the judge has no freedom at all. He cannot but echo the words of the law. The other extreme was the policy of Gény's *président Magnaud et les bons juges de Chateau-Thierry*. These were kindly disposed judges who administered the law according to lofty ethical principles. Their business was platonic: the administration of justice without law. Neither extreme is acceptable. If discretion is conceived too narrowly, the judge cannot properly perform his judicial task. Discretion, without generally accepted criteria for its exercise, results in arbitrariness.

At present, discussions regarding discretion do not dwell on its desirability, for no one doubts that the courts *have* discretion. The open texture of law leaves to courts a law-creating power.[2] The court's decision is a final, authoritative statement of what the law is in a particular case.[3] This is the core of discretion.

What matters is how the courts use their discretionary powers. 'At any given moment, judges, even those of a supreme court, are parts of a system, the rules of which are determinate enough at the centre to supply standards of correct judicial decision.'[4] 'It is, of course, possible that behind the shield of the rules which make judicial decisions final and authoritative, judges might combine in rejecting the existing rules and cease to regard even the clearest Acts of Parliament as imposing any limits on their decisions.'[5] If the judges were to conspire in this way, they would desecrate the rule of law and the entire legal system. But this would turn against the judges themselves. When there is a clear, unequivocal and recent rule of law laid down by the legislature or a high court, a judge is bound to follow it. After all, a judge is not a maverick legislator and is not called to rule solely according to his own bias. The judge must do not more than the legal system permits him to. If reluctant to accept this proviso, he should look for another vocation.

The purpose of secondary rules is to define the contents of primary rules (*sc.* the rules of recognition). They also lay down procedures according to which the judge must ensure that both primary and secondary rules are enforced (*sc.* the rules of adjudication). If the judge fails to fulfil this task, the higher court can reverse. The legal system provides for remedies when the upper court judges fail. These remedies must be applied and executed by other officials. Their failure would mean the end. The moral integrity of the judicial officials is the ultimate guarantee that justice is done according to law. It is also the end of their discretion.

Edgar Bodenheimer finds it difficult to accept that Hart's exposition of discretion, on which the above argumentation is based, is unspecific in describing the limits of the judicial law-making discretion.[6] He implies that Hart should have elaborated a theory which allows us a line of demarcation between legitimate and illegitimate judicial innovation.[7] Bodenheimer proceeds to mention some criteria to solve that problem. But there is no need for that. The problem is formulated in an inaccurate way. There is a very clear criterion for legitimate judicial innovation. Civil procedure tells us all about it, offering the 'shield of the rules which make judicial decisions final and authoritative.' Another question than Bodenheimer's is relevant: which judicial innovation is desirable? Or, in other words, which judicial innovation is acceptable? (*Sc.* to society) The answer to that question is a matter of fact. It can be measured, because acceptance can be determined by empirical research. The reply depends upon the opinion of the individuals who are affected by the judicial innovation. Admittedly, there is more to say about this. The legal system and judicial tradition have set criteria to decide which kind of judicial innovation is tolerable. These criteria grow. In some periods, judicial restraint is applauded. In others, judicial activism is appreciated. Arguments for either policy are in the end depending upon the political convictions one holds. In the nineteen-thirties when the U.S. Supreme Court blocked a lot of New Deal programmes, many liberals favoured judicial restraint. In the Nixon episode, they argued in favour of judicial activism.

Whether a judge adopts a narrow or a broad view of the use of discretionary powers and where he draws the limits depends upon moral or psychological motives. This proposition will be worked out in chapter 6. In section 5.3, it will be argued that there are, in fact, no legal barriers limiting the scope of discretion. This argument will be based upon the analysis of one aspect of the legal system the author is familiar with, namely, the Dutch system. For the convenience of the reader who only wishes to follow the general reasoning and not bother to read the case in point, a summary follows in section 5.2.

5.2 SUMMARY OF 'COURTS AND CORPORATIONS'

The Dutch economy is traditionally a system of free enterprise. But, by now, so many legal provisions have come into existence that the freedom of doing business is continually diminishing. A codified curtailment is to be found in Book II of the Dutch Civil Code, which grants several authorizations, such as the right of employees to inquire into the affairs of the company; the establishment of an enterprise council authorizing employees to request information regarding the corporate policy and strategy; the act on financial statement (i.e. the prerogative to comment on financial statement). Anyone who is granted a right by this Book II D.C.C. may ask the court to implement his right, if necessary. The Enterprise Chamber of the Amsterdam Court of Appeal has original jurisdiction. The above acts, which are now incorporated in Book II D.C.C., were subject to heated discussion when they were introduced in Parliament. In the end, the Government and the parliamentary majority emphasized that the court must follow a policy of restraint. The court should refrain from administering the companies to be brought before the bench. Such a policy is generally accepted and considered to be self-evident. Only recently, the Minister of Justice took the initiative in justifying the court's policy. He did so in Parliament when discussing the revision of the act which dealt with the right to inquire into the company affairs. His argumentation is analyzed in the next chapter. It consists of four premisses.

1. 'The judiciary is independent. Independence means that there is no obligation to justify action. It is unacceptable that an independent court should tell a company what to do, without having to justify that command;' but precedents show that the courts not only tell companies, but also the Government and individuals what to do. The legislator has granted authority to the courts in particular matters of economic competition, to tell companies in detail what to do or not to do.
2. 'The courts must not issue instructions that are in fact dictates to follow a policy.' Since the recent dive of the economy, the Government has been subsidizing corporations. Sometimes it requires shares in return. If so, it obtains a say in the policy of the concern and sometimes gets the final say in the general meeting of shareholders, thus enabling itself to dictate the company's policy. If the executive branch of government can have this authority, there is no reason that the 'least dangerous branch' (*sc.* the judiciary) cannot have that same authority also.
3. 'The consequences of the court's meddling into the corporation's affairs may result in huge financial losses.' The courts are used to ruling decisions that may have ruinous results on a litigant's financial state of affairs.
4. 'Administrative courts are also not allowed to dictate a policy to the government.' A scrutiny of recent decisions of the Judicial Division of the Council of State, the highest administrative court, makes clear that it does not hesitate to order the national government or local government to follow a certain policy.

After further analysis of the legal rules the Enterprise Chamber of the Amsterdam Court of Appeal must enforce, the conclusion is drawn that the Court is legally in the position to administer all companies that are brought before it. If the Court wished to, it could even prescribe the conduct of Dutch business life through, for example, selected managers. It goes without saying that the Court would never take such a liberty. But why not? There are no legal barriers. The answer is obvious, but worth exploring. The Court does not do so *because it does not want to*. This limitation is, by its nature, not legal. It can only be explained psychologically.

5.3 COURTS AND CORPORATIONS

5.3.1 Introduction

The Dutch economic system of *free enterprise* implies the freedom of entrepreneurs – at present, rather the boards of management – to organise and direct business undertakings, a freedom that is continually being diminished. In this section, some forms of curtailment by the Government and the judiciary will be discussed. The Act on Economic Competition authorizes the Government to interfere with the entrepreneur's (hereinafter referred to as member of the board of management, business manager, or manager) policy. The Act on Financial Statement, the Act on the Right to Enquire into the Affairs of the Company and the Act on the Enterprise Council (by now, all these acts are incorporated in Book II of the Dutch Civil Code) invest the Enterprise Chamber of the Court of Appeal of Amsterdam with original jurisdiction to tell the business manager what to do or not to do. When these acts came into existence warnings were issued that the Government or the courts must not take place on the chair of the board of management. That was considered to be incompatible with the roles the business manager, the administration and the court are supposed to perform. This section is devoted to the position of the court. It is generally assumed that the court carries an unbearable burden of responsibility when it is dealing with the manager's freedom of choosing a policy to direct business. This assumption is so widely accepted that no one bothers to reflect upon its plausibility. But there is an exception to the rule. The sometime Minister of Justice, Mr. Polak, once offered an argument in favour of this assumption when discussing in

Parliament the revision of the Act on the Right to Enquire into the Affairs of the Company. His reasoning is analyzed in the following sections.

5.3.2 The Holy Chair

The preamble of the Memorandum of Introduction of the Revision of the Act on the Right to Enquire into the Affairs of the Company contains the following thoughts.[8] In our economic system, where the production of goods and services is mainly an activity of privately owned concerns, the manager needs great freedom of action: it is he who decides – within the framework of our society – which goods will be produced by his company and it is up to him to choose the means and methods. Great freedom of action requires a high sense of responsibility towards those who place their labour or money at the company's disposal. It is safe to assume that, in general, the Dutch business manager has a proper sense of responsibility. But this does not disentitle that a legal system that meets the requirements of our economic system from being able to enquire into a company's affairs if there is doubt about the company's policy, and to take action when that doubt is justified. Such a warrant is given by the so-called Right to Enquire into the Affairs of the Company. The proposed draft for a parliamentary bill aims at an improved regulation.

The Social and Economic Council[9] has recommended that the Enterprise Chamber of the Amsterdam Court of Appeal should be granted authority to prescribe to the business manager a policy backed by a sanction. The then Minister of Justice, Mr. Polak[10], did not follow this advice.[11] His line of argument was as follows:

> This is not because I regard the entrepreneur's chair as being something sacrosanct, I do not recollect ever having said so. On the contrary, I think I have always maintained that this chair is anything but holy to me. How little I deem that chair to be holy, clearly follows from this very draft of act, which, after all, authorizes the court to dismiss members of the board of management and liquidate the company. I do not intend to support the entrepreneur in case of mismanagement. I am only concern-

ed that the court must not be thrust upon a body that is accountable to no one. According to the majority of the Social and Economic Council the court should be given authority to impose a policy, which the board of management is reluctant to adopt. According to this draft (*sc.* for a parliamentary bill) the board of management itself should have to decide which policy must be followed. Suppose the board of management is unwilling to adopt a particular policy and the reasons governing its refusal are, in the court's opinion, not wholly unjustified. If the court would feel differently, it has sufficient reason to replace the board of management. Consequently, it must be a case where the board of management's point of view is not totally unsound. How could the court ever assume responsibility for such a policy? What is the situation if the court ignores warnings from the board of management, but the latter is proved to be right and the company suffers losses or may even be ruined? Incidentally, it is, in general, not the task of the court to issue orders in matters relating to policy, if that policy does not originate from a legal obligation or a contract. In administrative law, too, the court can only nullify a wrong decision, but cannot issue a substitute if the original decision is concerned with matters that are legally within the discretion of governmental or administrative bodies. I think this is quite right, because otherwise one would not only curtail discretion in matters of policy, but would also thrust a responsibility upon the court that it could not bear, since it is an outsider that is accountable to no one.

5.3.3 The Minister's Argumentation

The argumentation of the Minister comes down to the following.

1.1. The courts are independent, that is to say, they are accountable to no one.

1.2. An independent court must not dictate a policy, for the substance of which it is not accountable.

2. It is outside the task of the courts to prescribe a policy, if the defendant is not obliged to follow it because of a contract or because of the law.

3. The results of the court's policy may constitute a financial catastrophy for the corporation. The court cannot afford to bear such responsibility.

4. (*Per analogiam*) In administrative law, the court is only authorized to nullify a wrong decision of a governmental or administrative body. It cannot replace the decision by one of its own, if that body, legally speaking, has discretion to follow a particular policy.

The reasoning sounds convincing, but is on bad terms with the present Dutch legal system. In fact, it is incompatible with it. The five paragraphs which follow refute the Minister's argumentation, the most fundamental aspect of which is the supposition that the courts are accountable to no one. This will be dealt with in paragraph 5.3.4, the other aspects being more circumstantial.

5.3.4 Accountable Courts

A Dutch judge is independent.[12] This means that other branches of government do not meddle in the court's affairs. They do not impose their will on the judge, nor do they exert influence upon his decision-making process. They respectfully obey the court's orders. Decisions that do not arouse the enthusiasm of the government are not supposed to have any influence on the judge's career. A consequence of judicial independence is that the judge is in the position to be inspired only by society's fundamental principles and values and that he tries to make his decisions in accordance with those basic standards as well as in harmony with the legal system.

Being accountable for decisions has four implications. *First*, it means that an explanation is required as to why and how the decision has been made. In the Netherlands, the judge has an obligation to motivate his decision.

Secondly, the judge must make his decision *acceptable*. The litigants must perceive that their arguments have been heard and understood and that they have been weighed in a fair manner, that is, objectively and impartially. Fellow-lawyers must be satisfied that the decision fits into the legal system. Society at large must also find the decision acceptable. The efficacy of our legal system depends upon the extent to which the individual people freely and habitually obey its legal rules. In these two senses, the courts are fully accountable for their actions.

There is a *third* aspect of accountability, though, namely, *liability* for the payment of money or damages. The Dutch legal system acknowledges liability for activities of branches of government. Liability of the state for the court's mistake is controversial.[13] Liability for the purely judicial activities of the courts is widely rejected. When the courts do more than declare what the law is and act as administrators of corporations, there seems no reason to reject liability by the state. There is no need in this study to elaborate the various aspects of the controversy. Suffice it to say that the accountability of the courts is not to be understood as referring to financial liability only. Possible financial liability was not even considered when granting to the court the authority to shut down a corporation (Act on Economic Competition) or to dismiss members of the board of management (Act on the Right to Enquire into the Affairs of a Company).

The *fourth* implication of accountability is being answerable to a superior. Judicial decisions are open to *judicial* review. The upper court is answerable to no one. That does not make it unfit to give judgment. If one argued that it is only permissible to make decisions if there is a higher authority to account to, that would be logically impossible. There is an end to everything. Judicial review cannot go on forever. In addition, it would be the end of an independent judiciary. That cannot be the purpose of a Dutch Minister of Justice's reasoning. The Minister does not say so. He argues that the absence of a higher authority to account to is a sufficient reason for disallowing the courts to give judgments regarding the *policy* of the business manager. There are precedents, though, to show that the courts do have that authority already. They have been mentioned above. The courts have a statutory right to give such judgments. This proposition will be dealt with in the next paragraph.

5.3.5 Judicial Intervention in the Company's Policy

Positive law authorizes the court to order the board of management to follow a particular policy. The Act on the Right to Enquire into the Affairs of the Company gives interested parties[14] the right to request the Enterprise Chamber of the Amsterdam Court of Appeal to order an investigation of the policy and the affairs of a company. If the request is sustained and if the Enterprise Chamber decides, after a rapportage and a hearing, that there is mismanagement by the defendant, it can order a number of measures to be taken. The measures are specified by the law.[15] This limited specification is meant to prevent the court from following a policy at free will and imposing on the manager any measure that happens to please the court. The Minister of Justice (*sc.* Mr. Polak) clarified this in Parliament. He was concerned about the judge, who must not be given an authority that is alien to his position of independence, which implies being accountable to no one.[16] But the Enterprise Chamber has the authority to take measures dealing with the *consequences* of the above list of specified measures.[17] Hence, the *court* can take measures at free will as it pleases.[18] The range of measures that are, after all, at the disposal of the Enterprise Chamber of the Amsterdam Court of Appeal will be discussed in paragraph 5.3.9.

In the bill to change the Act on the Enterprise Council, that has been sent to Parliament, it is proposed to give the Enterprise Council the right to address the Enterprise Chamber of the Amsterdam Court of Appeal if the board of management ignores its advice regarding the company's policy in matters affecting the position of the employees. The bill proposes to grant the court authority to take a limited number of specified measures only. It is the court's task to promote problem-solving by the litigants themselves. The reason for this restriction of the court's authority is based on concern that the court might occupy the seat of the business manager. But again, there are precedents which curtail the board of management's freedom to make decisions. The Government is entitled by the Act on Economic Competition to take action against some cartels and some dominant market positions. When this act was discussed in Parliament, some members expressed their concern with respect to the legal certainty of the manager in relation to the Government. Parliament insisted on possibilities of control by the judiciary. The act passed Parliament after insertion of a number of measures, whereas the court was to supervise in a marginal way only, namely, to ascertain whether the Government's behaviour was justified from the viewpoint of general interest. The memorandum of introduction explained this limitation:

> The government cannot take action against forms of behaviour of the company that are definitely against general interest, such as ineffective means of production and refusals to sell. This must be accepted. The Government would assume a responsibility it could not bear, if it gave instructions to companies to remedy this.[19]

Why the Government cannot do so is not explained. The matter is obviously regarded as self-evident. But during the recent decline in the Western economies, the Dutch Government has given financial support to a number of companies. Sometimes the Government has insisted in return that all the shares in the company concerned should be deposited in a special non-profit foundation in which the Government has a leading interest. Such an action enables the Government to have a final say in the affairs of the company. Obviously, the Government is not afraid of the responsibility it thereby incurs.

The judiciary is entrusted with control of the Government's behaviour, as defined by the Act on Economic Competition. It is also authorized to take far-reaching decisions according to the Act on Economic Offences. The court may even order a company to close down. The Act on Financial Statement entitles the court to prescribe company policy. These precedents are consistent with present views regarding the company's role in contemporary society. Recently, Parliament decided that 'the company, and especially big business, has grown into a social institution that is accountable to interested parties.' The Act of Financial Statement imposes on the company a duty to inform interested parties about its financial policy. The Enterprise Council is entitled[20] to ask the Enterprise Chamber of the Amsterdam Court of Appeal to order the company to publish its financial statement exactly in accordance to the law. The same right is granted to the Amsterdam Attorney-General. The wording of the law allows discretion to the court and consequently it can follow a policy.[21] The way in which a company gives account of its policy *is itself an element of its policy.*

5.3.6 *The Policy of the Board of Management*

In section 5.3.2.1, the proposition was stated that it would not be the task of the courts to prescribe a policy, if the board of management and its members were not obliged to follow it because of a contract or the law.

According to article 2.8 D.C.C., the members of the board of management have a duty to manage properly. If they fail and the company is declared bankrupt, the official receiver will hear these members in accordance with article 2.138 and 2.248 D.C.C. According to article 1374 Section 3 D.C.C., all contracts must be executed in good faith. Therefore, the members of the board of management have certain obligations arising from their labour contracts with the company. One may argue that this legal obligation of proper management applies to the relation between the company and a member of the board of management. But a legal norm like this has a reflection upon other legal norms that are systematically interrelated with it. One may call that a *per analogiam* interpretation. When taking into consideration the wide connotation the Amsterdam Court of Appeal has given to the concept of 'interested party'[22] and the company's responsibility towards interested parties, one may presume that the members of the board of management also have the obligation to provide proper management for the benefit of interested parties, especially employees. A reasonable interpretation of article 2.8 D.C.C. and of the above labour contracts warrants the conclusion that interested parties may refer to these and demand at court that a member of the board of management or the board itself abstain from mismanagement. This part of the argumentation of the Minister of Justice, as paraphrased in section 5.3.2, is unsound. One may refute, though, that it may be true that the courts are authorized to intervene with the entrepreneur's discretion and policy, but that they cannot say which policy he must adopt. The borderline between these two categories is not a fixed one. Thus, this refutation is a verbal one only.

5.3.7 The Disastrous Results of Judicial Decisions

Some judicial decisions may have far-reaching consequences. A factory, for instance, may have one good selling product, which is the sole source of profit. If the court is persuaded to believe that the product is a patent infringement and the factory has to close down as a result, that judicial decision has financially disastrous results. The government sometimes has to obey a court order grudgingly. The decision in 1950 of the President of the District Court of The Hague to allow 13,000 South Moluccans to enter the Netherlands has had various consequences, among which the financial are not the most significant.[23] A President of a district court, hearing summary proceedings, may issue an injunction because of a trade-mark infringement. If that injunction prevents the promotion of a new product in which a multinational has invested huge amounts of money, the court order may result in gigantic losses. To sum up, the mere possibility that a judicial decision may result in financial disasters is not, nor should be, a reason to curtail thc court's jurisdiction. That is the way it is and always has been as long as judicial authorities have existed. The present array of measures of the Enterprise Chamber of the Amsterdam Court of Appeal may result in financial disasters. A safeguard against that is the standing, skill, ability and integrity of the justices of the court and their exercise of restraint. What is more, the Government has a distinctly positive influence upon the selection of these court officials before they are called to the bench. This part of the Minister's argumentation is unsound.

5.3.8 The Policy of the Courts

The Judicial Division of the Council of State[24] is authorized to declare the decision of a ministry or governmental agency null and void, if it is illegal or lacks proper motivation. If the Judicial Division feels that the decision is illegal, the ministry or governmental agency cannot but give a decision as indicated by the Judicial Division. Although the latter may only consider the illegality (or motivation), it supplies, in fact, an outline for the policy of the ministry or governmental agency in question: 'Taking the aforesaid into consideration the new decision should lead to granting the licence plaintiff asked for.'[25] The Council of State thus imposes, in fact, a policy upon the governmental body or agency.

R.M. Dworkin has made some illuminating observations about the policy of the judge.[26] He points out that the logic of a legal system and the judicial decision-making process imply that the judge has discretion when it comes to applying the law.[27] If a judge has the right of discretion, then he also to a certain extent becomes a policy-maker. Dworkin has also some pointed comments on the topics of judicial policy, judicial activism, and judicial restraint.[28] There is no need to discuss them here in detail. Only one aspect may be highlighted. Legislation by parliament is a decision of a majority about the rights of a minority. The courts have also the duty to maintain the rights of the individual against the government. In Western democracies, governments by and large represent the majority of society. The courts are called to administer the law and see that justice is done according to its precepts. The courts must help the individual by giving fair judgments, that is, impartial and objective, whereas this would be a quite unnatural activity for a government. The judges are trained to follow a policy that is meant to do justice. If one argues that the courts may not follow any sort of policy, that is the same as saying that they do not operate properly.

A plea for or against judicial intervention in the entrepreneur's policy cannot be supported by *legal* arguments, but only by *political* arguments. It depends on one's conception of the value of free enterprise. There may be *practical* reasons in favour of a judicial restraint regarding the business manager's policy. What are the judges up to? What can they handle? They are jurists, not managers. For this reason, some of the justices of the Enterprise Chamber of the Amsterdam Court of Appeal are jurists and others are experts in business administration.

5.3.9 The Policy of the Enterprise Chamber

Parliament expressly stipulated that the Enterprise Chamber of the Amsterdam Court of Appeal should not take measures amounting to a management policy. But, at the same time, Parliament enacted article 2.357 section 2 D.C.C. saying that the Enterprise Chamber of the Amsterdam Court of Appeal may determine, if necessary, the nature of the consequences resulting from its decision. The Enterprise Chamber takes measures in case of mismanagement. It is also the only judicial body entitled to declare whether mismanagement has taken place. If the Enterprise Chamber says that it has, then mismanagement becomes an established fact. No appeal against this decision is possible.[29] Hence, Parliament gives a loophole to the court to defy the expressed will of Parliament itself. What is the meaning of the expressed will of Parliament that does not filter into the Code? In Parliament, the then Minister of Justice, Mr. Polak, was quite unambiguous about this. The interpretation of the law, and especially civil law, must be left to the courts. The courts may conclude – quite rightly in this case, the Minister added – that no matter what observation the Minister has made, they had better disregard it if they consider it to be nonsensical.[30] The doctrine that opinions expressed in Parliament are at best nothing more than a clue to interpretation by the courts is generally adopted by the Supreme Court and the rest of the Dutch judiciary.[31] In paragraph 5.3.8, the difference between concepts and conceptions was mentioned. Conceptions are susceptible to change. An illustration is the change of attitude towards the forcible occupation of factories and business premises. In the nineteen-sixties, they were considered illegal *per se*. In the 'seventies' it became widely accepted that in certain circumstances a plant-occupation was not illegal. In the interpretation of company law, one can also perceive a change of attitude concerning acceptable norms and patterns of behaviour relating to employers versus employees. Behaviour that was acceptable ten years ago, may now be unacceptable. What was proper management ten years ago, may now be considered to be a paradigm case of mismanagement, for example, the ignoring of these norms and patterns of behaviour. If the Enterprise Chamber of the Amsterdam Court of Appeal says that mismanagement has occurred because the norms have been violated, then mismanagement becomes a proven fact. This is a matter of judicial definition. In such a case, the Enterprise Chamber is authorized to dismiss the board of management and replace it by court-appointees. The Enterprise Chamber is thus entitled to determine what consequences shall be the product of its decisions! The newly-appointed managers may be instructed to follow a certain policy and to submit reports weekly. If a sufficient number of interested parties brought a sufficient number of companies to court, the bulk of Dutch business life might be managed by the Enterprise Chamber of the Amsterdam Court of Appeal. It is most unlikely that this would ever happen, *because the justices of this court would certainly not want to.* Such a wish is an example of pragmatism. This conclusion is not as provoking as it may appear to be. This situation is always there when a so-called empty concept[32] is the crux for a court order. In every case, the Enterprise Chamber looks at what the relevant conception is regarding mismanagement. It tries to find out the decisive criteria as set out by business life, business schools, unions, politics, *etc.* This is the core of the judicial decision-making process aiming to achieve acceptable decisions.

5.3.10 Non-Legal Limitations to Judicial Discretion

What is it that makes judges observe limitations to their discretion? The judge has a lot of options. He may take a great variety of decisions that are all covered by the shield of legitimacy, since they are in harmony with civil procedure.

The late professor Paul Scholten, the Dutch legal theorist, observed: It is the general human tendency to imitate, to follow; it is also the need we all have to learn from the judgment of others.[33] In addition, he pointed out the conserving influence exercised by the judge's desire to prevent his decision from being quashed by a higher court. Scholten suggests that the judge feels obliged to contribute to legal certainty.

Professor Langemeijer once used the term 'legal conscience'[34], meaning a tendency to operate with and within the legal system. It is the acceptance of the role which the law and the legal system play in our society. It implies a silent acknowledgement of the integrity of other decision-makers outside the judge's realm, such as politicians and administrators, for example. It is an acceptance of the fact that social and political conditions are continually changing and must change. The judge's 'legal conscience' is related to the acceptability of judicial decisions. If the judge wishes acceptance, he must know where he should stop exerting his judicial powers. He must pay head to the maxim: 'every man to his trade.'

In section 5.3.9, it was argued that the Enterprise Chamber of the Amsterdam Court of Appeal is authorized to take any measure affecting the management of a corporation that is brought before the bar. In the light of what has been said earlier in this paragraph, that observation is exaggerated. The Enterprise Chamber may legally do as it pleases and as long as it shields its love of interference with the legitimacy that legal procedure can offer. But, *in fact*, it cannot vouchsafe itself such freedom. The tether of the court is acceptability before a threefold audience consisting of the litigants, the fellow-lawyers and society at large. The end of this restraining tether is of a non-legal character. In section 5.4, this topic will be further explored.

5.3.11 Conclusion

The basis of the Dutch economic system is free enterprise. But the business manager's freedom is steadily diminishing. The administration and the courts can order the board of management what to do or not to do. Seemingly, the court has only moderate means of interfering with the board of management's policy. This limitation has always been justified by the self-evident assumption that the court should not be burdened with a responsibility it cannot bear. The former Minister of Justice, Mr. Polak, once offered arguments in support of this justification - a justification that does not hold. The courts, especially the Enterprise Chamber of the Amsterdam Court of Appeal, can, in fact, interfere with the company's management as they please. Limitations to the court's authority to do so are of a non-legal character.

5.4 PSYCHOLOGICAL AND MORAL LIMITATIONS TO DISCRETION

So far, it has been extensively argued that the borders of the judge's discretion are defined by non-legal factors. It remains to be seen why judges keep within the *legal* boundaries of their discretion. They do so by their own choice. One may presume that the judge's black robe and the trapping of the courtroom elevate him into a position of responsibility which will ensure the proper administration of the law. This observation is not an adequate explanation for the phenomenon that judges in Western legal systems advocate the ideal of fairness, that is, impartiality and objectivity. What is the driving force that makes them act accordingly? This study is not a treatise on psychology. A psychological explanation will be ventured, though. C.G. Jung's theory is illuminating here. Jung insists that the concept of *persona* elucidates people's relations and aspects of their behaviour.[35] People have in public life a certain way of presenting themselves. A doctor, for instance, has good bedside manners and behaves as one would expect a doctor to behave. He must correspond to an accepted image, otherwise people will not believe he is a doctor. The *persona* is a complicated system of behaviour which is dictated by the demands of society and partly by the fictitious image one has of oneself. That is the case, for example, if the doctor identifies himself with the role and believes what it appears to be. The *persona* is the mask of the individual; it is a compromise between the individual and society about what the former appears to be.[36] The *persona* is not the real personality. Every individual has his *persona*, the product of his function in public life. The *persona* is inspired by general expectations of others who belong to this environment. In Western societies, people have very definite expectations as to what a judge should be like. According to Jung's theory the judge habitually assumes the role, the attitudes and values of his judgeship and may make them his own. The *persona* becomes a prominent personal aspect of the judge. It depends upon the personality of the judge in how far his individuality dissolves into his *persona*. The effects of role performance upon the individual have been the object of several studies.[37] There has been much speculation about the influence of a person's occupation on his or her personality. As far as I have been able to ascertain, the only study which attempts to examine the judge's personality is a modest and hardly alarming paper entitled *Changes in Magistrate's Attitudes During the First Year on the Bench.*[38] The changes are not significant so far as views on the substance or goals of law are concerned, but, regarding procedural aspects of the legal system and role performance, the contrary was found to be true.

The conclusions from the above consideration sound like a conservative, common-sense statement: the judge is guided by such qualities as impartiality, learning, reasonableness and integrity *because he is expected to be*. Rohde and Spaeth contend:

> Possession of these attitudes is difficult to demonstrate. What one person conceptualizes as an indicator of impartiality, another may perceive as bias. Learning may appear to be sophistry to one group and lack of common sense to another. One person's understanding of integrity may appear to be compromise to others. Consequently, recourse is had to devices that inculcate respect and reverence. This age-old tactic of mankind effects acceptance and belief with a minimum of inquiry or examination.
>
> The essence of reverence and respect is a ritualized pattern of behavior. For judges, this has come to include the distinctive garb of a black robe, the occupancy of a seat elevated above the level occupied by others, the dispensation of justice surrounded by the ornaments of pomp and circumstance, and the use of oral and written discourse largely unintelligible to the layman. When he is off the bench, a judge is expected to be a faceless member of his community, not readily recognizable as a participant in any non-judicial activity. Though judges constitute an integral part of the political process, they are expected to avoid participation in partisan politics. In both public and private life, the judge should epitomize the moral ideas of his community.[39]

The power of society to outline the judge's behaviour and to enforce compliance seems to be strong enough to ensure the required conformity. The tendency to compliance is not to be conceived as just a personality treat.[40] Blessed be the nation where the 'ideal' judge, by whom the judge must be inspired, is the Completely Adult Jurist as pictured by Jerome Frank.[41] Society moulds its judges, thus securing that they keep in line. Hence, the psychological limitations to judicial discretion are set out by prevailing moral and political views in society. The judge may exercise his discretion as far as it is acceptable to society and to his legal peers (*sc.* to ascertain that it fits into the legal system).

Incidentally, this theorizing on psychology and C.G. Jung's observations relating to the *persona* may be helpful in highlighting another aspect of the judicial process. It is a peculiar fact that, whereas at a certain time in history a particular topic may cause heated debate, some time later that same topic bothers nobody at all. The explanation may be that the topic has no longer any relevance, since the issue has been settled. An example of this is the controversy about whether the earth is round or flat. But sometimes the explanation is not so easy. In the U.S.A., there is considerable discussion about the abolition of the death penalty. In the Netherlands, for example, that issue has already been settled and no one who argues that the death penalty should be restored is taken seriously. He is simply ignored. A legal scholar would even be ostracized if he pleaded in favour. Why this is so, is difficult to ascertain. There are, after all, arguments *pro* and *contra*. But nowadays the common opinion in the Netherlands is that the death penalty is unacceptable. Another example is the quite lenient attitude of Dutch courts towards squatters. A decade or two ago these invaders of private property were frowned upon, whereas nowadays, the courts show understanding for their actions and try to conciliate the squatters' interests and those of the property owners.

There is not always a rational explanation of the reasons why some ideas are picked up, prevail and are abandoned successively. This phenomenon of a silent *consensus* on certain themes bears some similarities with fashion, which is not simply a superficial feature of life, but constitutes an important regulator and means of expression in the community.[42] Fashion may also prevail amongst the ideals of a group. The 'feeling of being in harmony with fashion gives man a measure of security religion can never give him.'[43] The prevailing views the judge deems necessary to adopt, be it deliberately or subconsciously, are, and must be, in line with contemporary conceptions. The fashionable views, attitudes, ways of thinking, predilections, *etc.* one chooses presumably depend upon the *persona* one selects. The progressive lawyer defending left-wing radicals is attracted to a different *persona* than the big law-firm partners handling anti-trust cases. The role one adopts dictates modes of behaviour and thinking.

This proposition holds *vice versa*. The fashionable, generally accepted ideas of society and of the judges are reflected in their attitudes. As argued in section 2.1, these can be identified.

At the beginning of this section it was mentioned that the *persona* is a complicated system of behaviour, which is dictated by the demands of society and partly by one's fiction of oneself. Among those demands are requirements to observe certain moral values. A judge in Western societies must speak the law which is acceptable to his threefold audience (see sections 2.1.4.4 and 6.2.3). In order to do justice, he must respect the fundamental moral values of his society. In other words, it is a built-in characteristic of the judge's *persona* to observe the set of moral values that are related to a conception of justice (see section 2.2).

From this we may conclude that the limitations to the judge's discretion are dictated by his *persona*. Hence the limitations to discretion are ultimately marked by moral values.

CHAPTER 6. LOGIC AND 'NEW' RHETORIC

6.1 LIFE OF LAW IS EXPERIENCE, NOT LOGIC

In the 19th century, there were legal theorists who insisted that law was to be conceived as something like an axiomatic system. Once the system was set up, a few deductions would suffice for the judge to find the rule of law in a particular case. Legal certainty was supposed to be imminent. A codification and some experience with the principles of (Aristotelian) logic was all that was needed. This opinion, so typical for a time in which thought without roots in reality was held in high esteem, has become obsolete. The unrealistic approach was rebuked by Holmes when he said:

> The life of the law has not been logic: it has been experience. The felt necessities of the time, the prevalent moral and political theories, intuitions of public policy, avowed or unconscious, even the prejudices which judges share with their fellow-men, have had a good deal more to do than the syllogism in determining the rules by which men should be governed. The law embodies the story of a nation's development through many centuries, and it cannot be dealt with as if it contained only the axioms and corollaries of a book of mathematics.[1]

This point has been made in a blunter manner by Felix Cohen:

> Rules of logic...can no more produce legal or moral doctrines than they can produce kittens. On the whole, it is safe to assume that those legal doctrines that claim to be the offspring of logic are either not proud or not aware of their real parents.[2]

It is indeed a mistake to believe that logic can help us to find new law. Logic alone cannot be used to predict any event. The poorly understood use of logic as proclaimed by the 19th century philosophers has given logic a bad reputation among jurists. But modern logic may be so useful to legal practice that it would be a waste to leave it aside because of old misconceptions. Modern logic has enormous *analytical* powers. It can be used to analyse legal reasoning. It can serve to check whether a particular line of reasoning is formally valid, that is, whether the conclusion follows from its premisses. In sections 6.3 and 6.4, some more applications of modern logic will be mentioned. Logic cannot tell us what the law should be, but it can tell us whether sound reasoning has been employed.

Legal reasoning has many aspects and logical soundness is only one of them. In this study, the purpose of juridical reasoning and decision has been to enhance the acceptability of the decision. The logical soundness of a decision is a prerequisite of acceptability, although it should be admitted that an occasional lapse in logical soundness does not demolish acceptability. It is submitted that acceptability is promoted by the use of 'new' rhetoric or *zetetic*. An investigation of the different types of rhetorical reasoning is attempted in section 6.2. This investigation is not a guide to the application of rhetoric in the courtroom. Such aid is offered, for example, in *Art of Advocacy* by Lawrence J. Smith.[3] The relation between logic and zetetic is of a complementary nature. Logical soundness is a *conditio sine qua non*, which condition can be ascertained *after* the decision is about to be made. Some kinds of zetetic are, on the other hand, related to the tactics that are necessary to achieve a certain goal. For judicial reasoning, that goal is acceptance in the first place, preferably obtained through conviction and acceptable persuasion. When Aristotle wrote his *'Art' of Rhetoric*[4] which deals with an important part of zetetic, he paid much attention to the analysis of the personality of the one who is being spoken to. Zetetic has a direct link with an integral part of the substance of the case and of the character of the decision-makers. They are decisive for the zetetic strands that must be applied. They may even be decisive for the building up of the case, since rhetorical necessity may urge the speaker to underscore some facts and ignore others.

6.2.1 Introduction

Ilmar Tammelo's recent book *Modern Logic in the Service of Law*[5] contains an appendix which provides a conceptual articulation of legal reasoning in general.[6] This articulation supplies useful points of orientation also for forensic reasoning. By reference to the conceptual scheme of the author, an examination is proposed of certain kinds of reasoning that frequently can be found in situations at bar.

Tammelo divides legal reasoning into logical and zetetic.[7] Logical reasoning is deductive - in it the conclusion follows necessarily from its derivation basis.[8] If the premisses are true, the truth of the correctly derived conclusions is beyond any doubt. Zetetic reasoning can reach only conclusions that are beyond reasonable doubt.[9] These two kinds of legal reasoning are complementary in the sense that a lawyer uses both in the total context of his reasoning. The choice of which of the two and at which point he uses them depends on the aim he has in mind and on the position he is in.

This section contains only observations on kinds of zetetic reasoning which the judges and the advocates use. The legal reasoning of legislators, corporate lawyers or lawyers rendering legal advice is not considered here. A great number of even the best lawyers seldom go to court. They earn their living by negotiating for their clients and by advising them to behave in such a way that they keep out of court. Their legal reasoning is basically the same as that of the judge or the advocate. Legal reasoning in the court tends to be vivid and is the prototype of legal reasoning.

6.2.2 A Classification of Zetetic Reasoning

Tammelo divides zetetic reasoning by recourse to neologisms considered by him indispensable in order to achieve semantically adequate terminology for the purpose in view. A basic division is between reasoning that strives for probability, namely, exoduction, and that which aims at plausibility, namely, endoduction. The latter class is divided into *euduction*, by which the audience can be convinced and *perduction*, by which the audience can only be persuaded. About euduction he says:

> The essential feature of euductive procedures lies in the application of rules whose observance promotes impartiality, detachment, integrity, clarity, and intelligibility of the fact-situation and the value-situation relevant to the cases of application of euduction.[10]

About interduction and reduction, into which he divides exoduction, Tammelo observes:

> The interductive procedures...are concerned with the gaining of a statement about a datum from a statement about another datum, namely on the basis of the similarity which exists between these two data. In reduction, the thought moves from a particular to a general or from a less general to a more general; in interduction, the thought moves from a particular to another particular or from a general to an equally general.[11]

Thus, euduction on the one hand and reduction and interduction on the other belong to different categories. The former rests on the manner in which reasoning should be performed, while the latter rest on the patterns of reasoning. Both categories are concerned with the progress of reasoning. Reduction and interduction indicate the route, whereas euduction the means of transportation.

Tammelo does not include in his scheme the argumentative behaviour he calls 'seduction,' because the seductive procedures

> are not suited to secure the truth or tenability of claimed conclusions. Their machinations include logical fallacies and contentually irrelevant persuasion tricks actuated by deceitful intention.[12]

However, if a scheme of legal reasoning is to be descriptive of legal reality, seduction must be included as a common occurrence of the lawyers' argumentative behaviour. When a judge or an advocate opens his mouth, he does not wish to say that he is *probably* right. He claims that he *is* right. If possible, he renders a deduction that ends in a conclusion that can be claimed to be necessarily true. If not, he still claims that he is right and makes efforts to frame his reasoning in the most *plausible* or efficient way. Consequently, the reasoning of judges and advocates is above all logical, euductive, or perductive. It will be argued here that it may be seductive, too. The controlling question of this article is which kinds of zetetic reasoning are mostly used or are supposed to be used by judges and advocates. The role of a judge and an advocate in a legal system is different. Before their actual way of reasoning is discussed, a brief outline of their position in the legal system and in its law-applying processes is given.

6.2.3 The Judge

In our Western legal systems, the judge is supposed to give a decision that is fair, that is, impartial and objective. He must make clear that he has heard the arguments of the parties who have come to him. He must weigh those arguments and must balance the interests of the parties involved. If the law is clear, the judge is not concerned about the acceptability of his decision. He should, nevertheless, give a fair decision and make clear to the parties why and how he came to his conclusion. The law is seldom clear. From the facts presented to him by both parties involved, the judge selects the (legally) relevant facts and tries to subsume then under a legal rule. When the judge fails to find an applicable legal rule covering the selected facts and when rearrangements of the facts do not produce better results, the judge has to conclude that he is not competent to decide the case. This does not happen very often. Usually the judge is able to find his way through the case at bar.

The judge must link his decision to the legal system by means of a reasoning which is logically sound and which operates with true or tenable premisses. His decision and the reasoning supporting his decision should be given in such a way that both parties can understand that their arguments and claims have been scrutinized and weighed. The balance of pros and cons must be in favour of the winning party and the losing party must be provided with the reasons why he has lost his case. In general, the judge must make his decision *acceptable*. This acceptability is not only for the parties involved. Other lawyers who operate with and within the legal system must also be in a position to understand the outcome of lawsuits. They, too, must find that the decision is well-founded and thus acceptable. And the community at large must find the judicial decision acceptable. It is not contended that every layman, who might be subject to court jurisdiction, must understand and appreciate all judicial decisions. Some legal matters are too complicated or too specialized for that. But where court decisions eventually affect the man in the street, they ought to be acceptable.

In so far, the court has a political responsibility. U.S. courts have the tendency to recognize that responsibility. In controversial cases, anyway, they are aware of the public perception of the court and of the effect of the decision on society. A recent example is U.S. Supreme Court No. 76-811, Regents of the University of California *v*. Bakke. This decision partly satisfied most people and dissatisfied only a few. A wrong decision would have caused serious unrest in the U.S. The judge should realize that the bulk of the legal rules must be habitually obeyed by a large majority of the people. The efficacy of a legal system depends mainly on its acceptance by the public and not so much on the means to enforce the law. The possibilities of enforcing people's behaviour are limited. The point of acceptability is particularly raised in one particular kind of cultural climate. In a rigid society, where both nature and the social order are explained by a totalitarian view, the use of argument and acceptability of the contents of a decision are not great. There are formal criteria to check judicial decisions. The problem of argument is raised when people are basically in an equal position and try to influence each other's behaviour by means of words and do not settle terms at gunpoint.

In raising the question as to whom a judicial decision should be acceptable, three categories were mentioned: the parties involved (that is, the litigants), fellow-lawyers, and the community at large. These three audiences differ in structure and quality.

a. The Parties Involved: These must feel satisfied that justice has been done. I am inclined to the view that anything that promotes this objective is to be done by the judge. As far as the litigants are concerned, a judicial decision may even be seductive. But the judge should be careful. A triumph merely by seduction may produce a backfire and have an unfavourable effect on the public appraisal of the court.

b. Fellow-lawyers: These are capable of investigating the logical or zetetic soundness of the reasoning, the truth or tenability of the premisses, the goals of the legal system, the consistency of the judicial decision in relation to the legal system, the desirability of the given solution to the case at bar, and the like. Ideally, the judicial decision must fit into the pattern of deduction and it should be as convincing as possible. The assent of fellow-lawyers who have gained insight into the decision is the aim. Euductive procedures are the means of reaching this aim.

c. Society at Large: This audience is in itself heterogeneous. Judicial 'statesmanship' is required from the judge, who should realize the impact of his decision. This, of course, is not a matter of concern when non-controversial cases are at bar. But when a controversial issue has to be dealt with, the wisdom of the judge is needed. Usually the supreme court is more often asked to decide such cases than lower courts. The burden of responsibility is somehow lifted from the lower judge's shoulders merely by the possibility of appeal against his decision. But sometimes lower judges can also be called for decisions with far-reaching and irrevocable consequences. It would be too demanding to ask that a judge ought to produce a decision to the effect that his whole audience assents with insight or even with understanding. It would do to render a decision persuasive to everyone addressed, trying to assure also that reasonable men would agree that a benevolent and competent judge could come to this decision. This means that, for society at large, perductive reasoning is usually all that is required.

A judicial decision involves a mixture of several kinds of reasoning. It is intended to influence a mixed audience. Some premisses will appeal to one part of the audience, others to another part. By no means may the seductive premisses occur in the parts of reasoning which are intended for others than the litigants. The reasoning as a whole must meet standards of logical soundness and proceed from true or tenable premisses. Incidental seductive premisses in the reasoning must not be given the opportunity to get awry. These precepts hold for our Western legal system, in which the judge is historically a vital part of legal thinking. If two parties disagree, they have the possibility to go to court and obtain a fair decision. That possibility alone creates rules for behaviour. In civilizations which have not known Alexander's solution to a Gordian knot, a judge as we have it is an alien creature. In Indonesia, for instance, there has always been the institution of *mushawara*. All parties involved as well as their friends and relatives persist with discussion until unanimous agreement is reached. This means, of course, intriguing and negotiating and exercising influence. In such a system, it is natural that the judge can be influenced privately. An agreement there is never final. If the position of the parties changes, so does the agreement. Neither a contract, nor a judicial decision are the final words in a matter. The quality of a judicial decision meets different standards than it does in Western legal systems. In a civilization that embodies mystique in its legal system, causality and logic are not what we think they are. Under Western eyes, the key word for judicial reasoning in such a legal system is 'seduction.'

6.2.4 The Advocate

The role of the advocate is of uncertain nature. Roughly, there are two views about this role. Some see an advocate as 'one skilled in circumvention of the law.'[13] In the same view, 'lawful' means the will of a judge having jurisdiction.[14] This may sound cynical to those who hold a different view of the advocate's role. In any event, the advocate occupies an important position in a legal system. He represents the interests of his clients. He knows the law, he knows the work at bar and he is supposed to help the judge to make the proper decision. An advocate has a lofty position as far as he is a gentleman promoting justice. But he is also a businessman. When he has a sound reputation and an excellent standing, he is in a position to pick up the best cases and to collect considerable fees. When he is wealthy, he is independent and in the situation to accept only those cases which he thinks sufficiently worthy for him to represent. Nowadays, most advocates earn their living from legal practice. The better their reputation, the more they earn and the more comfortable their life can be. An advocate always bears in mind his client's interests and his own. Ideally, by promoting the interests of his clients, the advocate promotes his own interests. But the two do not always coincide.

After this indication of the threefold position in which an advocate finds himself, a distinction must be drawn between the kinds of court at which the advocate acts in a case and between the kinds of case in which he acts. A trial by jury gives the advocate the opportunity to practice forensic rhetoric in a way that would cause Protagoras to rejoice. A cross-examination is a highly appreciated step in the defence of, or in the attack on, the litigants. An advocate should not deliberately lie, but for the rest, seductive reasoning is at his disposal. The judge has the duty to see that truth does not leave the courtroom. Neither is it the task of the advocate to present the relevant facts in a misleading manner. At the same time, it is his duty to frame his client's claim in the most favourable way possible. The borderline between misrepresentation of facts and a flattering representation is vague. Besides other criteria, an advocate takes into consideration whether the truth of his proposition can be discovered by the judge as a guideline in the way he presents his case at bar. A criminal trial tends to be emotionally more appealing than a civil litigation. An advocate bears this in mind when he looks for the most efficient arguments.

The interest or importance of a case at bar may also be important for choosing which way of reasoning is to be used. If a factory launches a new product with a new brand-name and is sued and if an injunction is obtained to stop the using of that brand-name because of infringements of an older trademark, the atmosphere of the case is somewhat catch-as-catch-can. Even a temporary interruption to a promotion campaign may jeopardize the promotion of the new product and damages may be disastrous for the factory. The defending advocate is requested to do his utmost. Seduction is at his disposal and the temptation to use that mode of reasoning is strong.

In general, the higher the court is the stricter the standards are that an advocate's reasoning must meet. If the nature of the case is specialized and the legal reasoning is rather technical, the advocate is most successful if his reasoning is formally impeccable. If the nature of the case is not specialized, the role of logical reasoning is not prominent; there is rather a succession of seduction, perduction and euduction. How and when these are used depends on the quality of the judge and on the quality of the advocates. When an advocate has a competent colleague acting for the other side of the case and when he addresses a competent and experienced judge, seductive reasoning may be a treacherous method. If an advocate's fallacies and misleading presentation of the facts are noticed, they spoil his cause. An advocate with a good reputation in a certain field of law who uses premisses which are manifestly incompatible with the recent court rulings on the subject damages his reputation and prejudices the case in which he is acting.

The possibility to use seductive reasoning is limited by the aloofness of other lawyers in the courtroom and by social control. The judge has an important function together with an advocate's opponent. They are the warrants that justice is done. They are on the spot to keep their fellow-lawyer in line. The efficacy of social control depends on the position of the advocate in a legal system and on the public perception of the social standing of lawyers. A lot of cases are settled outside the courtrooms before they need to be presented to the court. The main task for an advocate is to advise his clients and to try to keep them out of court, rather than to present a show of forensic reasoning. Some excellent lawyers dislike going to court as much as laymen do. What happens outside the law courts and inside law firms and business offices is influenced by the law-making activities in the courtrooms. A legal system is served well if the possibility of winning a case by means of seduction is not great and if euductive reasoning is the habitually used method of advocating.

6.2.5 Conclusion

Both advocates and judges use euduction, perduction, and seduction. Advocates are freer in the choice of their methods than judges, the latter having the obligation to serve public interest. What their choice will be, depends on the nature of the case at bar, the kind of court before which the case is brought and on the strength of the premisses that are available. Seduction may be very efficient, but for prudent lawyers it comes into question only as the last resort. Judges and advocates should first try to employ euductive reasoning. If this is impossible, they may try perductive reasoning. The distinction between the three modes of reasoning – euduction, perduction, seduction – can be drawn only in abstraction. In legal reality, they are mixtures as a rule and hardly ever found in their pure form.

6.3 A LOGICAL SCRUTINY OF THE VAN DUYN CASE

6.3.1 Introduction

In this section, an example is given of services which modern logic can render to law. Most legal reasoning need not be checked on its logical virtue. An experienced lawyer has the ability to identify inconsistencies and other flaws of reasoning intuitively or by relying on his common sense and logical judgment. But sometimes legal reasoning is complicated to the extent that even the finest 'feeling' for logic is not enough to determine whether that reasoning is logically sound. An illustration of this is provided in the Van Duyn Case - a leading case of the European Court of Justice.[15] It happens that sometimes even most skilful lawyers are led astray in formal intricacies of their arguments and fail to conform their reasoning to indispensable logical standards.[16]

Modern logic provides the lawyer with ways and means for tracing and displaying consistent thought.[17] In recent years, especially Austrian legal theorists of the Institute for Legal Philosophy of Salzburg have made concentrated efforts to lay foundations which would enable academic as well as professional lawyers to benefit from the services of modern logic.[18]

Despite the notable results of a world-wide intensive work on legal logic during three decades, many lawyers are still sceptical, even contemptuous, of the usefulness of logic in the service of law.[19] However, their qualms are unfounded. It is wrong to assume that the goal of modern legal logic is to frame law as an axiomatic system or to join in the mischief of *Begriffsjurisprudenz*. Modern logic is compatible with and indispensable for any rational approach to law. Its effect is not to put legal reasoning into a 'straight-jacket.' On the contrary, it makes transparent the essentially 'open structure of law' and indicates the 'leeways' available for judges which enable them to pass decisions required by moral or political considerations.

Sometimes lawyers think that logic is useful only for the operation of subsumption. This is not so. Logic has important tasks which go far beyond that operation in making legal thought amenable to rational analysis and construction. Some dismissals of logic in the service of law are based on the assumption that logic is still basically Aristotelian (syllogistic) logic.[20] This logic is, of course, inadequate for dealing with normative thought. In modern logic, syllogisms are only a special kind of inference among many other forms of inference which are of legal relevance. All summary objections to legal logic seem to ignore that modern (or symbolic) logic contains a set of instruments without which contemporary tasks of ethics and law cannot be performed in intellectual integrity.

A controversial case of the European Court of Justice – the Van Duyn Case – has been deliberately selected for the following analyses. Many critics have commented on it. In none of these comments was there a complaint about the logical soundness of the Court's reasoning. But the Court did fail to conform to logical standards. The merits of the case are left aside for the present purpose. In the sequel, the arguments of the Court will be checked mainly on their logical *validity* (that is, do the conclusions follow from their premisses?) and on their logical *solidity* (that is, are the premisses free from contradictions?). The method used to perform the corresponding tests is the Counter-formula Decision Procedure as provided by Ilmar Tammelo in his *Modern Logic in the Service of Law*.[21] First, an outline of this method will be supplied. The reader who is not familiar with modern logic need try to acquire only an impression of the method. Even though he may not be able to follow its application in detail, he should, nevertheless, be able to form an idea of the way in which modern logic works in dealing with the logical aspect of a case such as the present one.

6.3.2 An Outline of the Counter-Formula Decision Procedure

The subsequent analyses of the Van Duyn Case are carried out by means of propositional calculus. Since only a brief account of the Counter-formula Method (CFM) can be given here, the reader is referred for a detailed exposition of the method to *Modern Logic in the Service of Law*.[22]

The notation to be employed is the Polish Notation modified by the use of 'D' for the dejunctor ('only if...then...') and of ' – ', that is, a bar on top of letters, for the negator ('it is not that...'). The other operators are: 'C' for the subjunctor ('if...then...'), 'A' for the adjunctor ('...or...'), 'K' for the conjunctor ('...and...'), and 'E' for the bijunctor ('if and only if...then...'). Small (roman) letters of ordinary size (p, q, etc.) are employed for propositional variables, that is, for any proposition whatsoever - they occur in the present section. Small (roman) letters of reduced size are employed for propositional instances, that is, for determinate propositions - they occur in the formalizations of the Court's arguments.

The set of instruments of the CFM contains (1) transcription rules (T.R.s), (2) elimination rules (E.R.s), and the rule of position rearrangement (R.P.R.). T.R.s effect the expression of all compound formulas other than adjunctions or conjunctions either as adjunctions or as conjunctions. E.R.s make it possible to break down formulas into shorter ones. R.P.R. makes it possible that the components of formulas can be reorganised in a manner required by the application of the method.

For the present purposes, it will be sought to establish above all: (1) whether or not a conclusion is valid, that is, whether or not it necessarily follows from its derivation basis (that is, from its premiss or premisses), (2) whether or not a conclusion is solid, that is, whether or not its derivation basis is non-contradictory. The goal of the procedure is achieved either when the application of the relevant rules produces a counter-formula (CF) to any formula appearing in the derivation or when, after the exhaustion of all applicable rules, this proves to be unachievable. CF is a formula which differs from another formula by one bar on top of its first component. These formulas stand then in a formula-counterformula relationship (F-CF).

The transcription rules of the CFM are: (1) Subjunction Duality (S.Dual.), (2) Dejunction Duality (D.Dual.), (3) Bijunction Dissection (B.Diss.), (4) Contrasubjunction Duality (CS.Dual.), (5) Contradejunction Duality (CD.Dual.), (6) Contraadjunction Duality (CA.Dual.), (7) Contraconjunction Duality (CC.Dual.), and (8) Contrabijunction Dissection (CB.Diss.).

The elimination rules of the CFM are: (1) Double Negation (D.N.), (2) Autology (Aut.), (3) Conjunction Elimination (C.E.), (4) Conjunction Contraction (C.C.), (5) Adjunction Elimination (A.E.), and (6) Adjunction Contraction (A.C.).

The CFM is carried out in a pattern similar to that of ordinary deductive proofs. It contains a derivation column (on the left-hand side) and a justification column (on the right-hand side). The former contains the formulas belonging to the derivation basis and thereafter the further formulas required to provide a proof. The latter contains the abbreviations of the rules applied together with the number or numbers indicating the relevant entry or entries; it may also contain the abbreviation of counter-formula. The conclusion appears on the top of the justification column.

To prove whether or not a conclusion is valid, the counter-formula of the conclusion (CFC) is entered after the last premiss. If the application of the method produces a CF for any entry in the derivation column, the conclusion is valid. If all applicable rules have been exhausted and this result is not achieved, the conclusion is invalid. To prove whether or not a conclusion is solid, the rules of the method are directly applied to the formulas in the derivation basis. If all applicable rules have been exhausted and a F-CF cannot be established, the conclusion is solid. If, however, a F-CF appears, the conclusion is insolid.

The validity-invalidity and the solidity-insolidity proofs can be combined in a consolidated procedure. This starts with the latter kind of proof. If the solidity of the claimed conclusion is established, a line is drawn under the last entry of the derivation column. Below this line the validity-invalidity proof is carried out. The consolidated procedure avoids the need to repeat entries.

6.3.3 The Facts of the Van Duyn Case[23]

The following statement of the facts of the Van Duyn Case contains only those points which are essential for the present purpose. The leaders (...) indicate the parts of the case report which have been left out here.

> The Church of Scientology is a body established in the United States of America, which functions in the United Kingdom through a college at East Grinstead, Sussex. The British Government regards the activities of the Church of Scientology as contrary to public policy. ...Foreign nationals come to Britain to study Scientology and to work at the so-called College ... The British Government can prevent this under existing law ... and have decided to do so. The following steps were taken with immediate effect ...
> (e) Work permits and employment vouchers will not be issued to foreign nationals ... for work at a Scientology establishment.
>
> No legal restrictions are placed upon the practice of Scientology in the United Kingdom nor upon nationals (with certain immaterial exceptions) wishing to become members of or take employment with the Church of Scientology.
>
> 2. Miss Van Duyn is a Dutch national. By a letter dated 4 May 1973 she was offered employment as a secretary with the Church of Scientology at its college at East Grinstead. With the intention of taking up that offer she arrived at Gatwick Airport on 9 May 1973 where she was interviewed by an immigration officer and refused to enter the United Kingdom.

> The ground of refusal of leave to enter which is stated in the document entitled 'Refusal to Leave to Enter' handed by the immigration officer to Miss Van Duyn reads: 'You have asked for leave to enter the United Kingdom in order to take employment with the Church of Scientology, but the Secretary of State considers it undesirable to give anyone leave to enter the United Kingdom on the business of or employment of that organisation.'

Miss Van Duyn appealed to this decision before the High Court. This Court stayed the proceedings and requested the European Court of Justice to give a preliminary ruling. The Court was asked to answer three questions. Each of these questions will be stated and the arguments leading to the answers of them will be subjected to logical treatment in the following three sections.

6.3.4 First Question

The Question Submitted:

> By the first question, the Court is asked to say whether Article 48 of the EEC Treaty is directly applicable so as to confer on individuals rights enforceable by them in the courts of a Member State.

The Text of the Argument:

> It is provided, in Article 48 (1) and (2), that freedom of movement for workers shall be secured by the end of the transitional period and that such freedom shall entail 'the abolition of any discrimination based on nationality between workers of Member States as regards employment, remuneration and other conditions of work and employment.'
>
> These provisions impose on Member States a precise obligation which does not require the adoption of any further measure on the part either of the Community institutions or of the Member States and which leaves them, in relation to its implementation, no discretionary power.
>
> Paragraph 3, which defines the rights implied by the principle of freedom of movement for workers, subjects them to limitations justified on grounds of public policy, public security or publiuc health. The application of these limitations is, however, subject to judicial control, so that a Member State's right to invoke the limitations does not prevent the provisions of Article 48, which enshrine the principle of freedom of movement for workers, from conferring on individuals rights which are enforceable by them and which the national courts must protect.
>
> The reply to the first question must therefore be in the affirmative.

The Logical Structure of the Argument:

In structuring the argument of the Court for the purpose of its logical treatment, its above expression will be re-worded by resorting to an interpretation which will bring out the gist of the argument. The logical words expressing the operators will be italicised. After each propositional component a letter (in reduced size) which is to represent this component in the formalisation of the argument will be added in brackets.

> *If* there is the end of the transitional period (e) *then* freedom of movement for workers shall be secured (f). *And if* f *then it is not that* there is a discrimination based on nationality between workers of Member States as regards employment, remuneration and other conditions of work and employment. (d)

This part of the argument can be expressed by

(1) Formula: $KCefCf\bar{d}$

> There is a precise obligation imposed on Member States which does not require the adoption of any further measure on the part of the Community institutions (i) *and* there is a precise obligation imposed on Member States which does not require the adoption of any further measure on the part of Member States (s). *And if* i *and* s *then it is not that* there is for the Member States discretionary power in relation to implementation of either obligation (p).

(2) Formula: $KKisCKis\bar{p}$

> There is Paragraph 3, which defines the rights implied by the principle of freedom of movement for workers (t) *and if* t *then* there is a Member State's right to invoke limitations of the rights implied by the principle of freedom of movement for workers (l).

(3) Formula: $KtCtl$

> *If* l *then* there is judicial control on the limitations of the rights implied by the principle of freedom of movement for workers (j) *and if* j *then if* l *then* Article 48 confers on individuals rights that are enforceable by them (o) *and* Article 48 confers on individuals rights which the national courts must protect (n).

(4) Formula: $KCljCjClKon$

The ruling of the Court:

> Article 48 of the EEC Treaty has a direct effect in the legal orders of the Member States (m) and n.

(5) Formula: Kmn

The first four formulas are the premisses and the last formula is the conclusion of the Court's argument. It is obvious that the argument with this conclusion is invalid, provided that it is solid, for m does not appear in any of its premisses. If, however, m is regarded only as an expression of an explanatory statement and n is taken to be the essential part of the Court's ruling, it is worthwhile to subject the argument to a logical test by the CFM.

Consolidated Solidity and Validity Proof:

1.	$KCefCf\bar{d}$		
2.	$KKisCKis\bar{p}$		
3.	$KtCtl$		
4.	$KCljCjClKon$	/.·.	n
5.	$A\bar{e}f$		1, C.E., S.Dual.
6.	$A\bar{f}\bar{d}$		1, C.E., S.Dual.
7.	$A\bar{e}\bar{d}$		4,5, A.C.
8.	Kis		2, C.E.
9.	i		8, C.E.
10.	s		8, C.E.
11.	$CKis\bar{p}$		2, C.E.
12.	$A\bar{K}is\bar{p}$		11, S.Dual.
13.	$AA\bar{i}\bar{s}\bar{p}$		12, CC.Dual.
14.	$\bar{p}$		13,9 & 13,10, A.E.
15.	t		3, C.E.
16.	Ctl		3, C.E.
17.	$A\bar{t}l$		16, S.Dual.
18.	Clj		4, C.E.
19.	$A\bar{l}j$		18, S.Dual., D.N.
20.	$CjClKon$		4, C.E.
21.	$A\bar{j}A\bar{l}Kon$		20, S.Dual.

22. l		17,15, A.E.
23. AjKon		21,22, A.E.
24. Ajo		23, C.C.
25. Ajn		23, C.C.
26. AoA$\bar{l}$Kon		24,21, A.C.
27. AoA$\bar{l}$o		26, C.C.
28. Ao$\bar{l}$		27, R.P.R., Aut.
29. o		28,22, A.E.
30. AnAlKon		25,21, A.C.
31. AnA$\bar{l}$o		30, C.C.
32. j		19,22, A.E.
33. AnA$\bar{l}$n		30, C.C.
34. An$\bar{l}$		33, R.P.R., Aut.
35. n		34,22, A.E.
Solid:	F-CF unattainable	
36. $\bar{n}$		CFC
Valid:	35,36: F-CF	

This test proves that the Court's argument relating to the First Question is solid: the derivation basis of the conclusion contains no contradiction. It also proves that the argument is valid, because the procedure produced a formula and its counter-formula. The test further shows that Premisses 1 and 2 are redundant for the purpose of the validity proof, because this proof can be provided without resorting to them.

6.3.5 Second Question

The Question Submitted:

The second question asks the Court to say whether Council Directive No. 64/221 of 25 February 1964 on the co-ordination of special measures concerning the movement and residence of foreign nationals which are justified on grounds of public policy, public security or public health is directly applicable so as to confer on individuals rights enforceable by them in the courts of a Member State.

The Text of the Argument:

It emerges from the order making the reference that the only provision of the Directive which is relevant is that contained in Article 3 (1) which provides that 'measures taken on grounds of public policy or public security shall be based exclusively on the personal conduct of the individual concerned'.

The United Kingdom observes that, since Article 189 of the Treaty distinguishes between the effects ascribed to regulations, directives and decisions, it must therefore be presumed that the Council, in issuing a directive rather than making a regulation, must have intended that the directive should have an effect other than that of a regulation and accordingly that the former should not be directly applicable.

If, however, by virtue of the provisions of Article 189 regulations are directly applicable, and, consequently, may by their very nature have direct effects, it does not follow from this that other categories of acts mentioned in that Article can never have similar effects. It would be incompatible with the binding effect attributed to a directive by Article 189 to exclude, in principle, the possibility that the obligation which it imposes may be invoked by those concerned. In particular, where the Community authorities have, by directive, imposed on Member States the obligation to pursue a particular course of conduct, the useful effect of such an act would be weakened if individuals were prevented from relying on it before their national courts and if the latter were prevented from taking it into consideration as an element of Community law. Article 177, which empowers national courts to refer to the Court questions concerning the validity and interpretation of all acts of the Community institutions, without distinction, implies furthermore that these acts may be invoked by individuals in the national courts. It is necessary to examine, in every case, whether the nature, general scheme and wording of the provision in question are capable of having direct effects on the relations between Member States and individuals.

By providing that measures taken on grounds of public policy shall be based exclusively on the personal conduct of the individual concerned, Article 3 (1) of Directive No. 64/221 is intended to limit the discretionary power which national laws generally confer on the authorities responsible for the entry and expulsion of foreign nationals. First, the provision lays down an obligation which is not subject to any exception or condition and which, by its very nature, does not require the intervention of any act on the part either of the institutions of the Community or of Member States. Secondly, because Member States are thereby obliged, in implementing a clause which derogates from one of the fundamental principles of the Treaty in favour of individuals, not to take account of factors extraneous to personal conduct, legal certainty for the persons concerned requires that they should be able to rely on this obligation even though it has been laid down in a legislative act which has no automatic direct effect in its entirety.

If the meaning and exact scope of the provision raise questions of interpretation, these questions can be resolved by the courts, taking into account also the procedure under Article 177 of the Treaty.

Accordingly, in reply to the second question, Article 3 (1) of the Council Directive No. 64/221 of 25 February 1964 confers on individuals rights which are enforceable by them in the courts of a Member State and which the national courts must protect.

The Logical Structure of the Argument:

In structuring this argument for the purpose of logical analysis, the relevant statements of the Court will be so constructed that the conjunctors do not occur as the first operators of the premisses. This expedites the decision-procedure by avoiding a repetitious application of the C.E. rule.

There is Article 3 (1) of the Council Directive No 64/221 of 25 February 1964 on the co-ordination of special measures concerning the movement and residence of foreign nationals which are justified on grounds of public policy, public security or public health (d).

This part of the argument can be expressed by

(1) Formula: d

If d *then* measures taken on grounds of public policy or public security shall be based exclusively on the personal conduct of the individual concerned (m).

(2) Formula: Cdm

It is not that there are regulations according to Article 189 of the Treaty (r).

(3) Formula: $\bar{r}$

It is not that there are directives according to Article 189 of the Treaty (i).

(4) Formula: $\bar{i}$

It is not that there are directives according to Article 189 of the Treaty (e).

(5) Formula: $\bar{e}$

If i *then it is not that* the directive is directly applicable so as to confer on individuals rights enforceable by them in the courts of a Member State (a).

(6) Formula: $Ci\bar{a}$

It is not that if a *then if* r *it is not that* a .

(7) Formula: $\bar{C}aCr\bar{a}$

If e *then it is not that* a .

(8) Formula: $Ce\bar{a}$

It is not that if i *then* a *and if* i *then it is not that* a .

(9) Formula: $\bar{K}CiaCi\bar{a}$

The Community authorities have, by directive, imposed on Member States the obligation to pursue a particular course of conduct (o).

(10) Formula: o

If individuals were prevented from relying before their national courts on the obligation of Member States to pursue a particular course of conduct (p) *and the* national courts were prevented from taking into consideration as an element of Community law the obligation of Member States to pursue a particular course of conduct (n) *then* the useful effect of the imposing on Member States to pursue a particular course of conduct would be weakened (w).

(11) Formula: $CKpnw$

There exists Article 1977, which empowers national courts to refer to the Court questions concerning the validity and interpretation of all acts of the Community institutions, without distinction (u).

(12) Formula: u

If e *then* the acts of the Community institutions may be invoked by individuals in the national courts (v).

(13) Formula: Cev

It is necessary to examine, in every case, whether the nature, general scheme and wording of the provision in question are capable of having direct effects on the relations between Member States (q).

(14) Formula: q

There is the provision of Article 3 (1) of Directive No 64/221 that lays down an obligation which is not subject to any exception or condition (f).

(15) Formula: f

There is the provision of Article 3 (1) of Directive No. 64/221 which, by its very nature, does not require the intervention of any act on the part either of the institutions of the Community or of Member States (g).

(16) Formula: g

There is an obligation of the Member States to implement a clause which derogates from one of the fundamental principles of the Treaty in favour of individuals, not to take account of factors extraneous to personal conduct, legal certainty for the persons concerned (x).

(17) Formula: x

If x *then* legal certainty for the persons concerned requires that they should be able to rely on this obligation even though it has been laid down in a legislative act which has no automatic direct effect in its entirety (t).

(18) Formula: t

If f *then* g *and* x *then* Article 3 (1) of Directive No 64/221 is intended to limit the discretionary power which national laws generally confer on authorities responsible for the entry and expulsion of foreign nationals by providing that measures taken on grounds of public policy shall be based exclusively on the personal conduct of the individual concerned (l).

(19) Formula: l

If the meaning and exact scope of the provision raise questions of interpretation (b) *then* these questions can be resolved by the courts, taking into account also the procedure under Article 177 of the Treaty (c).

(20) Formula: Cbc

Article 3 (1) of Council Directive No. 64/221 of 25 February 1964 confers on individuals rights which national courts must protect (z).

(21) Formula: z

The last formula represents the conclusion of the Court's argument; the formulas preceding it represent its premisses.

Solidity Proof:

1. d
2. Cdm
3. $\bar{r}$
4. $\bar{i}$
5. $\bar{e}$
6. $Ci\bar{a}$
7. $\bar{C}aCr\bar{a}$
8. $Ce\bar{a}$
9. $\bar{K}CiaCi\bar{a}$
10. o
11. CKpnw
12. u
13. Cev
14. q
15. f
16. g
17. x
18. t
19. l
20. Cbc /∴ z

21.	$A\bar{d}m$	2, S.Dual.
22.	m	21,1, A.E.
23.	$Ka\bar{C}r\bar{a}$	7, CS.Dual.
24.	a	23, C.E.
25.	Kra	23, C.E., CS.Dual., D.N.
26.	r	25, C.E.
27.	$A\bar{C}ia\bar{C}i\bar{a}$	9, CC.Dual.
28.	$AKi\bar{a}Kia$	27, CS.Dual., D.N.
29.	$AKi\bar{a}i$	28, C.C.
30.	Aii	29, C.C.
31.	i	30, Aut.

Insolid: 4,31: F-CF

The test proves that the premisses of the Court's argument contain a contradiction. According to the theorem of *Ex Falso Quodlibet*, any conclusion whatsoever follows as logically valid from a derivation basis that contains contradictions. Thus the conclusion of the Court's argument is valid. However, since under the same theorem the contradictory of this conclusion would also be valid, such a conclusion would be arbitrary. Supposing that the statements of the Court's argument would not contain any contradiction, the conclusion of the present argument would prove to be invalid, because it cannot be found in any logical connection among the premisses. This leads one to believe that a suppressed premiss is involved in the argument, which in the given form is enthymematic. This suppressed premiss, however, is not readily construable, which means that the Court has failed to provide a sufficient reasoning in dealing with the second question.

Some statements in the Court's argument could have been broken down into further propositions linked with logical operators. This would have not altered the result above reached, for a further logical articulation of the statements would have only yielded either repetition of formulas already gained or brought about new formulas. In neither case would the insolidity of the argument have been remedied. It is apparent that the conclusion of the argument would not have been contained in any of these new formulas.

6.3.6 Third Question

The Question Submitted:

By the third question the Court is asked to rule whether Article 48 of the Treaty and Article 3 of Directive No. 64/221 must be interpreted as meaning that

> 'a Member State, in the performance of its duty to base a measure taken on ground of public policy exclusively on the personal conduct of the individual concerned is entitled to take into account as matters of personal conduct:
>
> (*a*) the fact that the individual is or has been associated with some body or organization the activities of which the Member State considers contrary to the public good but which are not unlawful in that State;
>
> (*b*) the fact that the individual intends to take employment in the Member State with such a body or organization it being the case that no restrictions are placed upon nationals of the Member State who wish to take similar employment with such a body or organization.'

The Text of the Argument:

It is necessary, first, to consider whether association with a body or organization can in itself constitute personal conduct within the meaning of Article 3 of Directive No. 64/221. Although a person's past association cannot, in general, justify a decision refusing him the right to move freely within the Community, it is nevertheless the case that present association, which reflects participation in the activities of the body or of the organization as well as identification with its aims and its designs, may be considered a voluntary act of the person concerned and, consequently, as part of his personal conduct within the meaning of the provision cited.

This third question further raises the problem of what importance must be attributed to the fact that the activities of the organization in question, which are considered by the Member State as contrary to the public good are not however prohibited by national law. It should be emphasized that the concept of public policy in the context of the Community and where, in particular, it is used as a justification for derogating from the fundamental principle of freedom of movement for workers, must be interpreted strictly, so that its scope cannot be determined unilaterally by each Member State without being subject to control by the institutions of the Community. Nevertheless, the particular circumstances justifying recourse to the concept of public policy may vary from one country to another and from one period to another, and it is therefore necessary in this matter to allow the competent national authorities an area of discretion within the limits imposed by the Treaty.

It follows from the above that where the competent authorities of a Member State have clearly defined their standpoint as regards the activities of a particular organization and where, considering it to be socially harmful, they have taken administrative measures to counteract these activities, the Member State cannot be required, before it can rely on the concept of public policy, to make such activities unlawful, if recourse to such a measure is not thought appropriate in the circumstances.

The question raises finally the problem of whether a Member State is entitled, on grounds of public policy, to prevent a national of another Member State from taking gainful employment within its territory with a body or organization, it being the case that no similar restriction is placed upon its own nationals.

In this connexion, the Treaty, while enshrining the principle of freedom of movement for workers without any discrimination on grounds of nationality, admits, in Article 48 (3), limitations justified on grounds of public policy, public security or public health to the rights deriving from this principle. Under the terms of the provision cited above, the right to accept offers of employment actually made, the right to move freely within the territory of Member States for this purpose, and the right to stay in a Member State for the purpose of employment are, among others all subject to such limitations. Consequently, the effect of such limitations, when they apply, is that leave to enter the territory of a Member State and the right to reside there may be refused to a national of another Member State.

Furthermore, it is a principle of international law, which the EEC Treaty cannot be assumed to disregard in the relations between Member States, that a State is precluded from refusing its own nationals the right of entry or residence.

It follows that a Member State, for reasons of public policy, can, where it deems necessary, refuse a national of another Member State the benefit of the principle of freedom of movement for workers in a case where such a national proposes to take up a particular offer of employment even though the Member State does not place a similar restriction upon its own nationals.

Accordingly, the reply to the third question must be that Article 48 of the EEC Treaty and Article 3 (1) of Directive No. 64/221 are to be interpreted as meaning that a Member State, in imposing restrictions justified on grounds of public policy, is entitled to take into account, as a matter of personal conduct of the individual concerned, the fact that the individual is associated with some body or organization the activities of which the Member State considers socially harmful but which are not unlawful in that State, despite the fact that no restriction is placed upon nationals of the said Member State who wish to take similar employment with the same bodies or organizations.

The Logical Structure of the Argument:

Association with a body can itself constitute personal conduct within the meaning of Article 3 of Directive No. 64/221 (b) *or* association with an organization can in itself constitute personal conduct within the meaning of Article 3 of Directive No. 64/221 (o) *or it is not that* b (b) *or it is not that* o (o).

This part of the argument can be expressed by

(1) Formula: $AAboA\bar{b}\bar{o}$

It is not that a person's past association can, in general, justify a decision refusing him the right to move freely within the Community (d).

(2) Formula: $\bar{d}$

If the present association, which reflects participation in the activities of the body as well as identification with its aims, may be considered a voluntary act of the persons concerned (p_1) *or* the present association, which reflects the participation in the activities of the organization as well as identification with its aims, may be considered a voluntary act of the persons concerned (p_2) or the present association, which reflects the participation in the activities of the body as well as identification with its designs, may be considered a voluntary act of the persons concerned (g_1) *or* the present association, which reflects participation in the activities of the organization as well as identification with its designs, may be considered a voluntary act of the persons concerned (g_2), *then* this association with a body can in itself constitute personal conduct within the meaning of Article 3 of Directive No. 64/221 (c_1) *or* this association with an organization can in itself constitute personal conduct within the meaning of Article 3 of Directive No. 64/221 (c_2).

(3) Formula: $CAAp_1p_2Ag_1g_2Ac_1c_2$

If there is the concept of public policy in the context of the Community (l) *and* it is used, in particular, as a justification for derogation from the fundamental principle of freedom of movement for workers (j) *then* it must be interpreted strictly so that its scope cannot be determined unilaterally by each Member State without being subject to control by the institutions of the Community (s).

(4) Formula: $CKljs$

The particular circumstances justifying recourse to the concept of public policy may vary from one country to another (r_1).

(5) Formula: r_1

The particular circumstances justifying recourse to the concept of public policy may vary from one period to another (r_2).

(6) Formula: r_2

If r_1 *or* r_2 *then* it is necessary in this matter to allow the competent authorities an area of discretion within the limits imposed by the Treaty (n).

(7) Formula: CAr_1r_2n

The next proposition is a subjunction whose antecedent is the conjunction of the above propositions. To express it conveniently for the present purpose, each of them will be indicated by the number assigned to its formula. The first proposition, which is a tautology, can be discarded, since, being a logical truth, its statement is not necessary for the subsequent decision procedure.

If 2 *and* 3 *and* 4 *and* 5 *and* 6 *and* 7 *and* the competent authorities of a Member State have clearly defined their standpoint as regards the activities of a particular organization (t) *and* considering it to be socially harmful, they have taken administrative measures to counteract these activities (h) *then it is not that* the Member State can be required, before it can rely on the concept of public policy, to make such activities unlawful (u) *only if it is not that* recourse to such measure is thought appropriate in the circumstances (m).

(8) Formula:

$$\mathsf{CKKKKKKK\bar{d}CAAp_1p_2Ag_1g_2Ac_1c_2\text{-}}$$
$$\mathsf{CKljsr_1r_2CAr_1r_2nthD\bar{u}\bar{m}}$$

It is not necessary to formalize the next paragraph of the Court's reasoning, because it does not assert anything, but only expresses questions.

The Treaty, while enshrining the principle of freedom of movement for workers without any discrimination on grounds of nationality, admits, in Article 48 (3), limitations justified on grounds of public policy, public security or public health to the rights deriving from this principle (w).

(9) Formula: w

Under the terms of Article 48 (3), the right to accept offers of employment actually made, the right to move freely within the territory of the Member States for this purpose, and the right to stay in a Member State for the purpose of employment are, among others all subject to such limitations (i).

(10) Formula: i

If w *and* i *then if* there is a national of another Member State (a) *then* leave to enter the territory of a Member State and the right to reside there may be refused (f).

(11) Formula: $\mathsf{CKwiCaf}$

It is not that a State may refuse its own nationals the right to entry or residence (q).

(12) Formula: $\mathsf{\bar{q}}$

Only if for reasons of public policy a Member State can, where it deems necessary, refuse a national of another Member State the benefit of the principle of freedom of movement for workers (k) *then* this is in a case where such a national proposes to take up a particular offer of employment even though a Member State does not place a similar restriction upon its own nationals (v).

(13) Formula: Dkv

If there is a national of another Member State (x_1), *then* a Member State is entitled, on grounds of public policy, to prevent the taking of gainful employment within its territory with a body or organization (z).

(14) Formula: $C x_1 z$

If there is a national of the Member State itself (x_2), *then it is not that* a Member State is entitled, on grounds of public policy, to prevent the taking of gainful employment within its territory with a body or organization (z).

(15) Formula: $C x_2 \bar{z}$

The conjunction of the last two formulas represents the conclusion of the Court's argument. Since none of the small letters of this conjunction ($K C x_1 z C x_2 \bar{z}$) appears in the formulas representing the premisses of the argument (expressed by the preceding formulas), the conclusion of the present argument cannot be valid without being insolid and is therefore unsound. It remains now to be considered whether the Court's argument relating to the third question is at least solid.

In the analysis of judicial arguments, it often proves that they contain redundant premisses. It would simplify the solidity proof of the argument relating to the third question if the redundant premisses could be identified beforehand and thus eliminated for the purpose of the logical test. The following rule suggested by Helmut Schreiner would serve this purpose[24]:

For the purpose of validity or solidity tests, eliminate all formulas none of whose small letters occurs outside of the formulas employed as premisses of an argument.

In applying the rule of Schreiner, Formulas (12) and (13) can be eliminated. Since (1) as a tautology need not be employed either, the premisses for the following solidity proof are Formulas (2) to (11).

Solidity Proof:

1.	$\bar{d}$	
2.	$CAAp_1p_2Ag_1g_2Ac_1c_2$	
3.	$CKljs$	
4.	r_1	
5.	r_2	
6.	CAr_1r_2n	
7.	$CKKKKKKK\bar{d}CAAp_1p_2Ag_1g_2Ac_1c_2$- $CKljsr_1r_2CAr_1r_2nthD\bar{u}\bar{m}$	
8.	w	
9.	i	
10.	$CKwiCaf$ /.·.	$\underline{KCx_1zCx_2\bar{z}}$
11.	$A\bar{A}Ap_1p_2Ag_1g_2$- Ac_1c_2	2, S.Dual.
12.	$AKK\bar{p}_1\bar{p}_2K\bar{g}_1\bar{g}_2$- Ac_1c_2	11, CA.Dual.
13.	$A\bar{p}_1Ac_1c_2$	12, C.C.
14.	$A\bar{p}_2Ac_1c_2$	12, C.C.
15.	$A\bar{g}_1Ac_1c_2$	12, C.C.
16.	$A\bar{g}_2Ac_1c_2$	12, C.C.
17.	$AA\bar{l}\bar{j}s$	3, S.Dual., CC.Dual.
18.	$AK\bar{r}_1\bar{r}_2n$	6, S.Dual., CA.Dual.
19.	$A\bar{K}KKKKKK\bar{d}$- $CAAp_1p_2Ag_1g_2$- $Ac_1c_2CKljsr_1r_2$- $CAr_1r_2nthD\bar{u}\bar{m}$	7, S.Dual.
20.	$D\bar{u}\bar{m}$	19, 1-6, A.E.
21.	$A\bar{u}m$	20, D.Dual.
22.	$A\bar{K}wiA\bar{a}f$	10, S.Dual.
23.	$AA\bar{w}\bar{i}A\bar{a}f$	22, CC.Dual.
24.	$A\bar{a}f$	23, 8,9, A.E.

Solid: F-CF unattainable

6.3.7 Conclusion

The above analysis of the Van Duyn Case by means of the propositional calculus of modern logic and the examination of the arguments of this case by means of counter-formula method do not let the Court's reasoning appear as logically sound in all respects. It can scarcely be expected that resorting to finer logical tools such as those which predicational calculus (that is, the calculus which deals with the internal structure of sentences) supplies would lead to a different result. By reading into the case report thoughts which are not expressed there and by taking far-reaching liberties in the interpretation of the Court's statements, a logically sound reasoning could be produced - but this would mean writing a different judgment.

The authority of the Court's decisions depends on the total strength of the reasoning which the Court displays. Thus a logically defective reasoning renders the Court's performance in the present case unacceptable. To expose the logical defects of such a complicated case as the Van Duyn Case is not feasible by resorting to mere intuitive appraisals or to 'commonsense' logic. This can be done only by making use of the services of modern logic.

6.4 A COMPLEMENTARY SCRUTINY OF THE VAN DUYN CASE

Freedom of movement in the Common Market is acknowledged as a right. Pro-Marketeers boast about this EEC contribution to human rights. *Is* it a right? *Is* it to the benefit of the EEC citizen?

One can perceive migratory patterns in the Common Market that support the assumption that economic necessity forces migration in order to meet industrial demands for labour.[25] If there were no freedom of movement, capital would have to be invested where labour was available. That might be less economic, but would leave the social structures of migrant workers and their relatives more intact than in the situation we now have. By allowing millions of migrant workers to become estranged and bewildered, the human right of free movement contributes to social unrest all over Western Europe. The absence of this human right might encourage investment of capital where labour is abundant. That would provide for a more humane situation. It seems insincere to underscore the human rights aspect of the freedom of movement, but to ignore the economic convenience of it.

The Van Duyn Case has been criticized for various reasons. Amongst others, it is considered to incompatible with the right of free movement. It remains to be seen whether the outcome of this case is incompatible with the *ratio* of the free movement of workers. Governments of the Member States may dislike the presence of foreigners withing their territories, but are aware of the economic fact of life. Hence, they play host to tourists and accept migrant workers, if necessary. The economic realism of governments of Member States does not dissuade them from harassing individuals who do not belong to either category. Miss Van Duyn did not belong to either category. Incidentally, the United Kingdom entered the Common Market quite hesitantly. At that time, it would have been unwise from a political point of view to force the British authorities to allow entry to foreigners who were as unwelcome as the particular disciples of the Church of Scientology. The British public would not appreciate having to play host to followers of an organization regarded as contrary to the public good.

The Court of Justice has been unable to connect the politically desirable solution, as contained in the Van Duyn Case, to the legal system of the EEC by means of a logical and sound reasoning. But as far as judicial reasoning is concerned we cannot accept 'All's well that ends well'. It is dangerous to accept judicial decisions that are not supported by sound reasoning. The impact of judicial decisions may be immense, especially for those who are effected by it directly. It is unacceptable if a decision is not linked to the constitution, statutes, the body of expressed law and to the prevailing substance of law. That would leave room for arbitrariness.[26] There is logically no difference between the kind of reasoning resorted to in the Van Duyn Case and the following train of thought. Yes, freedom of speech does exist. But your opinion is undesirable, although not unlawful. You will be held in custody until you come round to a better way of thinking.

It is in this sense that logic, or rather logical analysis, can help to ensure that justice is done according to law. The traditional logical methods fail to bring to light the logical flaws of a complicated judicial reasoning as used in the Van Duyn case. The commonsense feeling for logic that lawyers have did not enable the many critics of the Court's decision to detect its logical defects.[27] Clearly the Court allowed itself to be used as an instrument of the unsound politics of Member States. If it was aware of this, that is no credit to the Court. If it was not, it is interesting to see how the error could have been prevented. Several times Holmes' adagium that law is the prophesying of the court's behaviour has been recalled. The court does not predict its own behaviour. It must apply the law on the basis of facts added to political or moral value judgments, thus allocating the burden its decision brings to a party. The court must make sure that the decision is consistent with the legal system. The Court of Justice did not follow this policy in the Van Duyn case, but gave way to an interpretation of legal rules and legal concepts by referring to other legal rules and legal concepts. The Court indulged in transcendental nonsense.[28] This means that practical questions are forgotten and that the judge takes refuge in legal problems which can always be answered by manipulating legal concepts in certain approved ways.[29] In order to ascertain the meaning of a rule of the EEC Treaty the Court should have considered what practical consequences might conceivably result from the authoritative interpretation it gives. The Court should have made this clear in the premisses of the reasoning.[30]

> A truly realistic theory of judicial decisions must conceive every decision as something more than an expression of individual personality, as concomitantly and even more importantly a function of social forces. A judicial decision is a social event. (...) Behind the decision are social forces that play upon it to give it a resultant momentum and direction; beyond the decision are human activities rendered by it. The decision is without significant social dimensions when it is viewed simply at the moment in which it is rendered. Only by probing behind the decision to the forces it reflects, or projecting beyond the decision of the lines of its force upon the future do we come to an understanding of the meaning of the decision itself. The distinction between 'holding' and 'dictum' in any decision is not to be discovered by logical inspection of the opinion or by historical inquiry into the actual facts of the case. That distinction involves us in a prediction, a prophesy of the weight that courts will give to future citations of the decisions rendered. This is a question not of pure logic but of human psychology , economics and politics.[31]

The Court of Justice gave a judgment that certainly failed to meet the above criteria. It rendered an unacceptable decision. If it wishes its decisions to have impact, it should properly analyze the facts and interests that are at stake in the case at bar. Here it stumbled upon a political issue. It would have been appropriate if the Court had relied upon a public policy analysis. A proper analysis of the facts and not transcendental nonsense is the basis for an impact of court decisions.

EPILOGUE

The purpose of the last chapter on modern logic was to stress the subtitle of this book: Towards a Rational Judicial Process. A judicial decision must be able to withstand the test of logical scrutiny. Its conclusion should derive from its premisses which must not be contradictory. To avoid all misunderstanding, I must emphasize that modern logic cannot help us to come to any conclusion. It is a powerful tool, though, for checking whether a judicial reasoning is sound. A rational judge will check this for himself before he announces his decision. If he finds that his reasoning is unsound, he must rearrange his premisses. If that rearrangement is unsuccesful, it is his duty to reconsider his decision.

While drawing up his premisses and making his decision, the rational judge takes into account the zetetic that he may apply to secure *acceptability* of his decision. As we have seen, this criterion is vital for the efficacy of judicial decisions. (It should be remembered that the judge's audience is threefold: the litigants, fellow-jurists who are able to decide whether the decision fits into the legal system and society at large.)

We have seen from the discussion in chapters 4 and 5 that the judge has ample means of moulding the legal system in order to justify moral and political ends. This issue is, in fact, one of judicial discretion or, in other words, the limits of judicial powers. Here, too, the concept of acceptability applies.

A side-trip into the realm of psychology was made to explain why judges keep in line with the legal system at all. The explanation given obviously does not exclude compliance with the legal rules that compel judges to operate within the procedural confines of the court's sovereignty and not to stray outside the framework of the legal system.

The judicial process has two sides: an inner and an outer. The former was dealt with in the chapters on logic, zetetic and on the prediction of judicial decisions. The latter depends on the factual circumstance that the court is a branch of government *and* a guardian of the individual's rights. Here the topics of judicial restraint, judicial activism and judicial interventionism were discussed as well as the notion of acceptability, the latter having been used to decide which policy the courts should adopt to meet their social responsibilities.

It is worth repeating that the main responsibility of the courts is of a technical nature. It is their task to declare what the law is, thus putting an end to disputes in a final and authoritative way. Western civilization needs people who are able to cut Gordian knots. But the rational judge should realize that he is more than a trouble-shooter. He shares his part of the burden of government, and mainly does so when he declares what the individual's rights consist of.

The underlying legal theory is a pragmatic branch of positivism. This study enters a stage in the age-old controversy between positivism and natural law. It does so by defending H.L.A. Hart's concept of law against certain recent attacks.

This study has been inspired by two main questions relating to law (see section 1.5). The first arose when I was a law student and used to wonder whether the question *'What is the law?'* could be answered. The second came when I started to practice and, while handling cases, I naturally had to ask myself *'What will the court do!'* This treatise is an account of the way in which I tried to deal with these and related problems. Writing it down has been helpful to me. I hope that my views will serve a useful purpose, whether the reader agrees with them or not.

SUMMARY

This study is governed by the assumption that democracy is the most desirable of the existing forms of government for countries of Western origin. The judicatory plays a vital role in enabling the democratic form of government to survive. This role is highlighted, whilst an analysis of the judicial process is worked out. The inquiry is based on the precepts of a pragmatic and positivistic legal theory as outlined in the first chapter and amended in subsequent chapters. The judicial process is so complicated that no single theory can embrace all its features and implications. Hence, only some aspects of the judicial process are scrutinized.

It is argued that the judicatory should improve its performance as well as its impact. It can do so not only by enlisting help from the legislature, but also especially by adopting a different view of its own task and taking advantage of means that are already within each reach. Examples in point are offered. (Some are taken from the Dutch legal system, with which the author is familiar.)

It is submitted that the controlling guideline for the judge must be the *acceptability* of his decisions. The judge has a threefold audience: The litigants, other jurists whose concern it is that the decision should fit into the legal system, and society at large. The bench is the 'least dangerous branch' of government, but it *is* a branch of government. The courts should acknowledge this fact and act accordingly.

A scrutiny of the judicial process leads to the conclusion that the judge has a much wider discretion than is usually assumed. His limitations are partly legal, but ultimately moral or psychological. An explanation is ventured as to why the judge keeps in line with the legal system and its purpose and why he adheres to objectivity, impartiality, learning and integrity.

Analysing the judicial process enhances predictions as to the outcome of court cases, thus improving what is generally known as legal certainty.

Finally, the role of zetetic (*i.e.* perduction and eduction, or 'new' rhetoric) and logic are discussed. Those modes of reasoning which have rhetoric as their historical antecedent are a requisite for satisfying the threefold audience of the judge. Modern logic is a useful technique with which to analyze judicial reasoning and may help to ensure that justice is done. It brings any of the judge's predilections or prejudices to light and, in general, exposes unsound legal reasoning. An example is given of the way in which modern logic enables us to reach the heart of judicial reasoning, especially when the commonsense 'feeling' of logic with which experienced jurists are endowed proves to be of no avail.

ZUSAMMENFASSUNG

Diese Studie wird von der Annahme getragen, daß unter den bestehenden Regierungsformen die Demokratie die wünschenswerteste Verwaltungsform für die Länder der abendländischen Zivilisation ist. Die richterliche Gewalt spielt eine vitale Rolle, da sie der demokratischen Regierungsform das Überleben ermöglicht. Diese Rolle der Gerichte wird beleuchtet, wobei das richterliche Verfahren, das es ermöglicht zu Entscheidungen zu gelangen, analysiert wird. Die Untersuchung wird nach den Grundsätzen einer pragmatischen und positivistischen Rechtstheorie durchgeführt, wie sie im ersten Abschnitt erörtert und in den folgenden Abschnitten ergänzt wurde.

Das richterliche Entscheidungsverfahren ist so kompliziert, daß eine einzelne Theorie nicht alle seine charakteristischen Merkmale und Schwierigkeiten umfassen kann. Daher werden nur bestimmte Aspekte dieses Verfahrens genau untersucht. Es wird dargelegt, daß die richterliche Gewalt sowohl ihre Leistung wie auch ihren Einfluß erhöhen soll. Dies kann sie nicht nur mit Hilfe der gesetzgebenden Gewalt erreichen, sondern besonders auch, indem sie eine anderen Gesichtspunkt hinsichtlich ihrer eigenen Aufgaben und Mittel, die bereits zur Verfügung stehen, einnimmt. Beispiele werden angeführt (manche stammen aus dem niederländischen Rechtssystem, das dem Autor bekannt ist).

Die Richtschnur für die kontrollierende richterliche Funktion soll die *Annehmbarkeit* ihrer Entscheidungen sein. Der Richter hat ein dreifaches Auditorium: die Streitparteien, andere Juristen, deren Interesse es ist, daß die Entscheidung dem Rechtssystem entspricht, und die Gesellschaft im allgemeinen. Das Gericht ist der 'am wenigsten gefährliche

Zweig' der Staatsgewalt, aber es *ist* ein Zweig. Die Richter sollen dieses anerkennen und dementsprechend handeln. Die genaue Prüfung der richterlichen Entscheidungsverfahren führt zur Schlußfolgerung, daß der Richter eine viel breitere Urteilsmöglichkeit hat als üblicherweise angenommen wird. Ihm sind teilweise gesetzliche Schranken gesetzt, aber letzten Endes auch moralische oder psychologische. Es wird die Frage geklärt, weshalb der Richter dem Rechtssystem und dessen Zwecken genau folgt, und weshalb er Werten wie Objektivität, Unparteilichkeit, Wissenschaftlichkeit und Integrität anhängt.

Die Analyse der richterlichen Entscheidungsverfahren ermöglicht die Voraussage hinsichtlich des Ausgangs anhängiger Streitfälle, wodurch die Rechtssicherheit gefestigt wird.

Schließlich wird die Rolle der Zetetik (d.h. Perduktion und Euduktion, oder 'neue' Rhetorik) und Logik besprochen. Die Denkformen, die aus der antiken Rhetorik erwachsen, sind ein Erfordernis, um das dreifache Auditorium des Richters zu befriedigen. Die moderne Logik ist eine moderne Technik zur Analyse des richterlichen Gedankenganges. Sie kann möglicherweise sicherstellen, daß Recht geschieht. Sie bringt jede Voreingenommenheit und jedes Vorurteil des Richters ans Licht, und deckt im allgemeinen ein ungesundes juristisches Denken auf. Anhand eines Beispiels wird dargetan, wie die moderne Logik es ermöglicht, das 'Herz' des richterlichen Gedankenganges zu erreichen, besonders wenn das 'gesunde Empfinden' für die Logik, das erfahrene Juristen haben, fehlt.

SAMENVATTING

Dit onderzoek gaat ervan uit dat de democratie de meest wenselijke staatsvorm is voor landen met een Westers cultuurpatroon. De rechterlijke macht speelt een belangrijke rol bij de instandhouding van de democratie. Het gaat om deze rol bij de analyse van het rechterlijk besluitvormingsproces. Het wetenschapstheoretische kader van waaruit het onderzoek plaatsvindt is een pragmatische en positivistische rechtstheorie, welke wordt geschetst in het eerste hoofdstuk en waar nodig in daarop volgende. Intussen is het rechterlijk besluitvormingsproces te gecompliceerd dan dat het door één enkele theorie geheel kan worden omvat. Om die reden beperken wij ons tot slechts enige aspekten van dat proces.

De doelmatigheid van het functioneren van de rechterlijke macht kan verhoogd worden met hulp van de wetgever, maar vooral ook wanneer de rechter een andere visie op zijn eigen taakstelling aanneemt. Overigens kan hij reeds zijn voordeel doen met thans beschikbare middelen. Daarvan zijn voorbeelden gegeven, voor een deel ontleend aan het Nederlandse rechtsstelsel waarmee de auteur vertrouwd is.

Een belangrijk richtsnoer voor de rechter is de *aanvaardbaarheid* van zijn beslissingen. De rechter heeft een drievoudig gehoor: de procespartijen, juristen als degenen die kunnen beoordelen of de beslissing in het rechtstelsel past, en de samenleving. De rechterlijke macht valt te onderscheiden van de uitvoerende macht, echter niet te scheiden. Hun taken overlappen elkaar gedeeltelijk. De rechter dient dit in zijn overwegingen te betrekken.

Uit het onderzoek van het rechterlijk besluitvormingsproces volgt dat de rechterlijke vrijheid veel minder door vaste regels is ingeperkt dan gemeenlijk wordt verondersteld. Soms zijn die moreel of psychologisch van aard. Aldus wordt verklaard waarom de rechter zorgvuldig binnen het rechtstelsel blijft en daarmee verknochte waarden respecteert volgens beginselen van objectiviteit, onpartijdigheid, wetenschap en integriteit.

Een analyse van het rechterlijk besluitvormingsproces verhoogt de voorspelbaarheid van 's rechters beslissingen, waarmee de rechtszekerheid verhoogd wordt.

Tenslotte wordt de rol van zetetica (dwz. perductie en euductie of 'nieuwe' rhetorica) en logica besproken. Deze modi van redeneren, welke zijn terug te voeren op de antieke rhetorica, zijn nodig om het drievoudig gehoor van de rechter tevreden te stellen. Moderne logica is een nuttig instrument om de redenering van de rechter te analyseren. Zodoende kan zij ertoe bijdragen dat gerechtigheid geschiedt. Zij brengt voorkeuren en vooroordelen van de rechter aan het licht en, meer in het algemeen, onthult gebreken in juridische redeneringen. Met behulp van een voorbeeld wordt aangetoond dat wij met de moderne logica een juridische redenering ten gronde kunnen analyseren. Dat geldt in het bijzonder wanneer het intuitieve gevoel voor logica, dat ervaren juristen eigen is, tekort schiet.

BIBLIOGRAPHY

N.B. The names of the authors will be mentioned in the manner as printed on their works.

Aristotle.	'Art' of Rhetoric. Translated by John Henry Freese, London, *etc.*, 1947. [Loeb Classical Library, No. 193.]
Asser, C.	Handleiding tot de beoefening van het Nederlandsch burgerlijk recht, Algemeen Deel. By Paul Scholten, third edition by G.J. Scholten, Zwolle, 1974.
Becker, Theodore L., and Malcolm M. Feeley. (eds.)	The Impact of Supreme Court Decisions. Second edition, London, *etc.*, 1973.
Bickel, Alexander M.	The Least Dangerous Branch, The Supreme Court at the Bar of Politics. New York, 1962.
Bickel, Alexander M.	The Supreme Court and the Idea of Progress. New Haven, *etc.*, 1979.
Blühdorn, Jürgen.	Kritische Bemerkungen zu Theodor Viehwegs Schrift: Topik und Jurisprudenz. In: Revue d'Histoire du Droit, XXXVIII (1979), pp. 269-314.
Bodenheimer, Edgar.	A Neglected Theory of Legal Reasoning. In: Journal of Legal Education, 21 (1969), pp. 373-402.
Bodenheimer, Edgar.	Hart, Dworkin, and the Problem of Judicial Lawmaking Discretion. In: Georgia Law Review, 2 (1977), pp. 1143-1173.
Bodenheimer, Edgar.	Jurisprudence. Cambridge, Mass., *etc.*, 1979.
Böhning, W.R.	The Migration of Workers in the United Kingdom and the European Community. Oxford, 1972.
Bond, Rod A., and Nigel F. Lemon.	Changes in Magistrates' Attitudes During the First Year on the Bench. In: David P. Farrington, Keith Hawkins and Sally Lloyd-Bostock (eds.), Psychology, Law and Legal Process,

London, *etc.*, 1979. [Oxford Socio-Legal Studies.]

Byse, Clark, and Walter Gellhorn. Administrative Law. Sixth edition, Minneola, New York, 1974. [University Casebook Series.]

Cahn, Edmond. Skepticism in American Jurisprudence. In: Lenore L. Cahn (ed.), Confronting Injustice, London, 1967, pp. 269-280.

Cahn, Edmond. The Consumers of Injustice. In: Lenore L. Cahn (ed.), Confronting Injustice, London, 1967, pp. 5-15.

Cahn, Richard du. The Art of the Advocate. Harmondsworth, *etc.*, 1980. [Reprinted with revisions.]

Cardozo, Benjamin N. The Nature of the Judicial Progress. New Haven, *etc.*, 1977. [Reprinted from the 1921 edition.]

Cohen, Felix S. Transcendental Nonsense and the Functional Approach. In: L.K. Cohen (ed.), The Legal Conscience, Selected Legal Papers of F.S. Cohen, New Haven, 1960, pp. 33-76.

Copi, Irving M. Introduction to Logic. Third edition, London, 1971. [Reprinted from the 1961 edition.]

Denning, [A.T.]. The Discipline of Law. London, 1979.

Denning, [A.T.]. The Due Process of Law. London, 1980.

Duncan, Colin, and Brian Neill. Defamation. London, 1978.

Dunné, J.M. van, P. Boeles, and A.J. Heerma van Voss. Acht civilisten in burger. Zwolle, 1977.

Duynstee, F.J.M. Rechtspleging. In: Opstellen rondom het thema rechterlijke organisatie, bijeengebracht ter gelegenheid van het vijftigjarig bestaan van de Faculteit der Rechtsgeleerdheid van de Katholieke Universiteit Nijmegen, Deventer, 1974, pp. 35-57.

Dworkin, Ronald M. Taking Rights Seriously. London, 1977.

Dworkin, Ronald M. Seven Critics. In: Georgia Law Review, 11 (1977), pp. 1201-1267.

Edel, Abraham. Legal Positivism: A Pragmatic Reanalysis. [Paper submitted to the 1979 Congress of the Internationale Vereinigung für Rechts-und Sozialphilosophie, Bâle. Not yet published.]

Ehmke, Horst. 'Ermessen' und 'Unbestimmter Rechtsbegriff' im Verwaltungsrecht. Tübingen, 1965.

Encyclopedia of Philosophy, The — Ed. by Paul Edwards, New York, *etc.*, 1972. [Reprinted from the 1967 edition.] The following articles have been quoted: Stanley I. Benn, Democracy, Vol. 2, pp. 338-341; Stanley I. Benn, Equality, Moral and Social, Vol. 3, pp. 38-42; Max Black, Probability, Vol. 6, pp. 464-479; H.L.A. Hart, Vol. 4, pp. 418-420; Peter Laslett and Philip W. Cummings, Political Philosophy, History of, Vol. 6, pp. 370-387; Alasdair MacIntyre, Spinoza, Benedict (Baruch), Vol. 7, pp. 530-541.

Esser, J. — Grundsatz und Norm in der richterlichen Fortbildung des Privatrechts, Rechtsvergleichende Beiträge zur Rechtsquellen. Third edition, Tübingen, 1974. [Untersuchungen zur vergleichenden allgemeinen Rechtslehre und zur Methodik der Rechtsvergleichung, Bd. 1.]

Farrington, David P., Keith Hawkins, and Sally Lloyd-Bostock. (eds.) — Psychology, Law and Legal Process. London, 1979. [Oxford Socio-Legal Studies.]

Finch, John D. — Introduction to Legal Theory. Second edition, London, 1974.

Frank, Jerome. — Law and the Modern Mind. New York, 1931.

Frank, Jerome. — Fate and Freedom. New York, 1945.

Friedmann, W. — Legal Theory. Fifth edition, London, 1967.

Fromm, Erich. — Escape from Freedom. New York, 1941.

Fuller, Lon L. — The Morality of Law. Revised edition, New Haven, *etc.*, 1978. [Reprinted from the revised, second edition from 1969.]

Gaay Fortman, W.F. de — Enka-bezetting en vennootschapsrecht. In: Verzekeringen van vriendschap, Rechtsgeleerde opstellen aangeboden aan prof. mr. T.J. Dorhout Mees, Deventer, 1974, pp. 255-263.

Gatley, [J.]. — Libel and Slander, Seventh edition by Robert McEwen and Philip Lewis, London, 1974. [With first supplements to the seventh edition, 1979. The Common Law Library, No. 8.]

Guthrie, W.K.C. — The Sophists. Cambridge, 1971.

Hall, Peter. (ed.) — Europe 2000. London, 1977.

Harrison, Albert A. — Individuals and Groups, Understanding Social Behavior. Monterey, California, 1976.

Hart, H.L.A. — The Concept of Law. Oxford, 1961. [Clarendon Law Series.]

Hart, H.L.A. — American Jurisprudence Through English Eyes: The Nightmare and the Noble Dream. In: Georgia Law Review, 11 (1977), pp. 969-989.

Heemskerk, W.H. — Annotation of Hoge Raad 2 April 1976, Nederlandse Jurisprudentie 1977, 361.

Holmes, Oliver Wendell. — The Path of the Law. In: Oliver Wendell Holmes, Collected Legal Papers, New York, 1920, pp. 167-202.

Hugenholtz, W. — Hoofdlijnen van Nederlands burgerlijk procesrecht. Twelfth edition, by W.H. Heemskerk, The Hague, 1979.

Jackson, Robert H. — The Struggle for Judicial Supremacy, A Study of a Crisis in American Power Politics. New York, 1941.

Jacobi, J. — Die Psychologie von C.G. Jung. Zürich, 1945.

Jessurun d'Oliveira, H.U. — De meerwaarde van rechterlijke uitspraken, arrêts de règlement en precedenten. Deventer, 1973. [Pre-advies uitgebracht voor de Nederlandse Vereniging voor Rechtsvergelijking, No. 10.]

Kelsen, H. — Recht und Logik. In: Neues Forum, 19 (1965), pp. 421 *seq.*

Kiesler, Charles A., and Sara B. Kiesler. — Conformity. Reading, Mass., *etc.*, 1969. [Topics in Social Psychology.]

Klenner, Hermann. — [Review of] H.L.A. Hart, Der Begriff des Rechts. In: Deutsche Literaturzeitung, 96 (1975), pp. 609-613.

König, René. — The Restless Image, A Sociology of Fashion. Translated by F. Bradley, London, 1973.

Krech, David, Richard Crutchfield, and Egerton L. Ballachey. — Individual in Society. New York, 1962.

Langemeijer, G.E. — De bescherming van eer en goede naam in ons land. In: Nederlands Juristenblad, 36 (1961), pp. 89-95.

Langemeijer, G.E. — De gerechtigheid in ons vermogensrecht. Second edition, Zwolle, 1979.

Laqueur, Walter. — Terrorism, A Balance Sheet. In: Walter Laqueur (ed.), The Terrorism Reader, A Histori-

	cal Anthology, New York, *etc.*, 1978, pp. 251-267. [New American Library.]
Laswell, Harold and Myres S. McDougal.	Criteria for a Theory about Law. In: Southern California Law Review, 44 (1971), pp. 362-394.
Laun, Rudolf von.	Das freie Ermessen und seine Grenzen. Leipzig, *etc.*, 1910.
Lewis, Anthony.	The Profession of Law. In: International Herald Tribune, 28 July, 1971.
Llewellyn, K.	Some Realism About Realism. In: Harvard Law Review, 44 (1931), pp. 1222 *seq.*
Lloyd of Hampstead, [D.].	Introduction to Jurisprudence. Third edition, London, 1972.
Lorenzen, P.	Die Vollständigkeit einer unverzweigten Variante des 'analytischen' Entscheidungsverfahrens der klassischen Logik. In: Archiv für mathematische Logik und Grundlagenforschung, 18 (1976), pp. 19-22.
McDougal, Myres S.	Jurisprudence for a Free Society. In: Georgia Law Review, 1 (1966), pp. 1-19.
McGuire, William, and R.F.C. Hull.	C.G. Jung Speaking, Interviews and Encounters. London, 1978.
Merkl, Adolf.	Die Lehre von der Rechtskraft. Leipzig, 1923.
Merkl, Adolf.	Allgemeines Verwaltungsrecht. Vienna, *etc.*, 1927.
Meij, J.M. de	De vrijheid en de verantwoordelijkheid van de pers. Utrecht, 1975. [diss.]
Meijers, E.M.	Het kort geding. Zwolle, 1945.
Onrechtmatige daad	Ed. by H. Drion, Deventer, 1964.
Pannock, David.	Time to end this English amateur law making. In: The Guardian, 10 September 1979.
Paust, Jordan J.	International Law and Control of the Media: Terror, Repression and the Alternatives. In: Indiana Law Review, 53 (1978), pp. 621-677.
Paust, Jordan J.	The Concept of Norm: A Consideration of the Jurisprudential Views of Hart, Kelsen, and McDougal-Laswell. In: Temple Law Quarterly, 52 (1979), pp. 9-49.
Perelman, Ch., and L. Olbrechts-Tyteca.	The New Rhetoric, A Treatise on Argumentation. Translated by John Wilkinson and Purcell Weaver, Notre Dame, *etc.*, 1971.
Perelman, Ch.	The Idea of Justice and the Problem of

Argument. Translated by John Petrie, London, *etc.*, 1970. [Reprinted from the 1963 edition. International Library of Philosophy and Scientific Method.]

Philostratus, [Flavius], and Eunapius. The Lives of the Sophists. Translated by Wilmer Cave Wright, London, *etc.*, 1968. [Reprinted from the 1921 edition. Loeb Classical Library, No. 134.]

Popper, Karl R. The Open Society and Its Enemies. Fifth edition, Princeton, New Jersey, 1971, 2 Vols. [Reprinted from the 1966 edition.]

Portalis [J.E.M.] Discours Préliminaire. Le 24 thermidor an 8. [Reprinted at Amsterdam, 1948, copied from Recueil Complet des Travaux Préparatoires du Code Civil, par P.A. Fenet, Paris, Tome I.]

Pound, Roscoe. Law in Books and Law in Action. In: American Law Review, 44 (1910), pp. 12-36.

Pound, Roscoe. An Introduction to the Philosophy of Law. Second edition, New Haven, etc., 1978. [Reprinted from the 1954 edition.]

Ringhofer, Kurt. Strukturprobleme des Rechts. Vienna, 1966.

Roch, John P. Courts and Rights, The American Judiciary in Action. Second edition, New York, 1968. [Reprinted from the 1966 edition. Studies in Political Science.]

Rohde, David, and Harold J. Spaeth. Supreme Court Decision Making. San Francisco, 1976.

Russell, Bertrand. History of Western Philosophy, and its Connection with Political and Social Circumstances from the Earliest Times to the Present Day. Second edition, London, 1974. [Reprinted from the 1961 edition.]

Ryle, Gilbert. The Concept of Mind. Harmondsworth, *etc.*, 1966. [Reprinted from the 1949 edition.]

Sacksteder, William. Spinoza on Democracy. In: Eugene Freeman and Maurice Mandelbaum (eds.), Spinoza, Essays in Interpretation, La Salle, Ill., 1975. [Monist Library of Philosophy.]

Schenk, W. Het kort geding en zijn toepassing in Nederland. Deventer, 1976.

Schermers, Henry G. The European Court of Justice: Promoter of European Integration. In: The American Journal of Comparative Law, 22 (1974), pp. 444-464.

Schermers, Henry G. The Communities under the European Convention on Human Rights. In: Legal Issues of European Integration, 1978/1, pp. 1-8.

Schilfgaarde, P. van Van de naamloze en de besloten vennootschap. Third edition, Arnhem, 1976.

Smith, Lawrence J. Art of Advocacy, Summation. New York, 1978.

Stone, Julius. Legal Systems and Lawyers' Reasonings. Stanford. 1964.

Swaan, A. de Uitgaansbeperking en uitgaansangst. Amsterdam, 1979. [Inaugural lecture.]

Tammelo, Ilmar, and Helmut Schreiner. Grundzüge und Grundverfahren der Rechtslogik. Munich, 1974-1977, 2 Vols. [Uni-Taschenbücher, No. 412 and 685.]

Tammelo, Ilmar. Zur Philosophie des Überlebens, Gerechtigkeit, Kommunikation und Eunomik. Freiburg, *etc.*, 1975. [Reihe: Fermenta philosophica.]

Tammelo, Ilmar, and Gabriël Moens. Logische Verfahren der juristischen Begründung, eine Einführung. Vienna, *etc.*, 1976. [Forschungen aus Staat und Recht, No. 35.]

Tammelo, Ilmar. Von der Demokratie und darüber hinaus, Umrisse einer 'eukratischen' Regierungsform. In: Gerd-Klaus Kaltenbrunner, Rückblick auf die Demokratie, Gibt es Alternativen?, Munich, 1977.

Tammelo, Ilmar. Modern Logic in the Service of Law. Vienna, *etc.*, 1978.

Thibaut, John, and Laurens Walker. Procedural Justice, A Psychological Analysis. Hillsdale, New Jersey, 1975.

Thomas, Evan, and Raissa Silverman. Judging the Judges. In: Time Magazine, 20 August 1979.

Thucydides. History of the Peloponnesian War. Translated by Charles Forster Smith, London, *etc.*, 1969. [Loeb Classical Library, No. 108, Books I and II.]

Twining, William. Karl Llewellyn and the Realist Movement. London, 1973.

Understeiner, Mario. The Sophists. Translated by Kathleen Freeman, Oxford, 1954.

Viehweg, Theodor. Topik und Jurisprudenz, Ein Beitrag zur rechtswissenschaftlichen Grundlagenforschung. Fourth edition, Munich, 1969.

Weinberger, Ota.	Jenseits von Positivismus und Naturrecht. [Paper submitted to the 1979 Congress of the Internationale Vereinigung für Rechts- und Sozialphilosophie, Bâle. Not yet published.]
White, G. Edward.	The American Judicial Tradition, Profiles of Leading American Judges. Oxford, *etc.*, 1978. [Reprinted from the 1976 edition.]
Wiarda, G.J.	Drie typen van rechtsvinding. Zwolle, 1972.

NOTES

Notes to Prologue

1. Theodor Viehweg, Topik und Jurisprudenz, München, 1969. See also Jürgen Blühdorn, Kritische Bemerkungen zu Theodor Viehwegs Schrift: Topik und Jurisprudenz. In: Tijdschrift voor Rechtsgeschiedenis, Revu d'Histoire du Droit, (1970), especially p. 271: 'Die Topik ist eine "Techne des Problemdenkens".' A convenient summary of Viehweg's theory has been rendered by Edgar Bodenheimer, A Neglected Theory of Legal Reasoning, Journal of Legal Education, 21 (1969), pp. 381-382.
2. Felix S. Cohen, Transcendental Nonsense and the Functional Approach, Columbia Law Review (1935) reprinted in: L.K. Cohen (ed.) The Legal Conscience, Selected Papers of F.S. Cohen, New Haven, 1960, p. 33 *seq*.
3. Portalis, Discours Préliminaire, le 24 thermidor an 8. Reprinted at Amsterdam, 1948, p. 3. Copied from Recueil Complet des Travaux Préparatoires du Code Civil, par P.A. Fenet, Paris, Tome I, p. 453 *seq*.
4. *E.g.* the Treaty of Rome; the Universal Declaration of Human Rights.
5. Karl Popper, The Open Society and Its Enemies, Volume I, The Spell of Plato, Princeton, 1971, p. 125.
6. H.L.A. Hart, The Concept of Law, Oxford 1961.

Notes to Chapter 1. Democracy and Positivism

1.1 Popper's Approach

1. Quoted from Stanley I. Benn, Democracy, in: The Encyclopedia of Philosophy, New York-London, 1967, Volume 2, p. 338.

2. Quoted from Stanley I. Benn, *op. cit.*, p. 340.
3. Karl R. Popper, The Open Society and Its Enemies, Volume I, The Spell of Plato; Volume II, Hegel and Marx, New Jersey, 1971.
4. Stanley I. Benn, Nature of Political Philosophy, in: The Encyclopedia of Philosophy, *op. cit.*, Volume 6, p. 389.
5. Popper, *op. cit.*, Volume II, pp. 128, 129. The meaning of the term 'mere formal freedom' is legal freedom as opposed to economic or material freedom, which is, according to Marx, what really matters. *Op. cit.*, Volume II, p. 124.
6. Popper, *op. cit.*, Volume II, p. 131.
7. Popper, *op. cit.*, Volume II, p. 124.
8. Popper, *op. cit.*, Volume I, p. 113.
9. Popper, *op. cit.*, Volume II, pp. 131, 132. The following lines are quotations from, and paraphrases of the, author's reasoning on p. 132.
10. Popper, *op. cit.*, Volume II, p. 225.
11. Popper, *op. cit.*, Volume II, p. 227.
12. Popper, *op. cit.*, Volume II, p. 232.

1.2 Positivism and Pragmatism

13. *Cf.* H.L.A. Hart, Legal Positivism, in: The Encyclopedia of Philosophy, *op. cit.*, Volume 4, p. 419.
14. *Idem.*
15. At the present time, several scholars are trying to bury the ancient controversy. *E.g.* Ota Weinberger, Jenseits von Positivism und Naturrecht, paper submitted to the 1979 congress of the Internationale Vereinigung für Rechtsphilosophie, held in Bâle, Switzerland.
16. Abraham Edel, Legal Positivism: A Pragmatic Reanalysis, paper submitted to the IVR congress as mentioned above in note 15.
17. Edel, *op. cit.*, pp. 10 *seq.* The following is derived from Edel's argumentation too. *Cf.* also p. 28.
18. Edel, *op. cit.*, p. 28.
19. Edel, *op. cit.*, p. 28.
20. H.L.A. Hart, The Concept of Law, Oxford, 1961.
21. Lon L. Fuller, The Morality of Law, New Haven-London, 1978.

22. Ronald Dworkin, Taking Rights Seriously, London, 1977. A new impression has been published in 1978. The latter also contains an article entitled 'Seven Critics' which was published in Georgia Law Review, 11 (1977), pp. 1201-1269. There are certain slight differences between that article and the version in the 1978 edition of 'Taking Rights Seriously'.
23. *Cf.* John D. Finch, Introduction to Legal Theory, London, 1970, p. 67.
24. Professor Dr. Hermann Klenner, H.L.A. Hart, Der Begriff des Rechts, review of a translation into German by Alexander von Baeyer, in: Deutsche Literatur Zeitung, Berlin, 96 Jahrgang, Heft 7, July 1975, pp. 609-613.
25. Fuller, *op. cit.*, pp. 133 *seq.*
26. *Cf.* W. Friedmann, Legal Theory, London, 1967, pp. 352 *seq*: 'The case reported in 64 Harv. L. Rev. 1005 and the discussion of this case between Professor Hart and Fuller 71 Harv. L. Rev. 618 *et seq.* (1958) 652 *et seq.*'
27. Friedmann, *op. cit.*, p. 354.

1.3 Hard Theories and Hard Cases

28. Ronald Dworkin, Taking Rights Seriously, London, 1977.
29. Dworkin, *op. cit.*, p. 14.
30. Dworkin, *op. cit.*, p. 17.
31. Dworkin, *op. cit.*, p. 22.
32. Dworkin, *op. cit.*, p. 81.
33. Dworkin, *op. cit.*, p. 87.
34. Dworkin, *op. cit.*, p. 87.
35. H.L.A. Hart, American Jurisprudence Through English Eyes: The Nightmare and the Noble Dream, in: Georgia Law Review, 11 (1977), p. 984.
36. Dworkin, *op. cit.*, p. 9.
37. Dworkin, *op. cit.*, p. 31.
38. Adolf Merkl, Allgemeines Verwaltungsrecht, Vienna-Berlin, 1927, p. 196; Die Lehre von der Rechtskraft, Leipzig-Vienna, 1923, pp. 293, 297.
39. H.L.A. Hart, The Concept of Law, Oxford, 1961.
40. Dworkin, *op. cit.*, p. 45.
41. Dworkin, *op. cit.*, p. 45.

1.4 Standards: a Category-Mistake

42. Benjamin N. Cardozo, The Nature of the Judicial Process, London, 1977, p. 112.
43. Gilbert Ryle, The Concept of Mind, Harmondsworth, 1966, pp. 17-20.
44. Dworkin, *op. cit.*, p. 24.

1.5 Two Main Questions Relating to Law

45. *Cf.* Lord Denning, The Discipline of Law, London, 1979, pp. 197 *seq.*:

> The importance of the *High Trees* case, as I see it, is this: During the 19th century the Courts of Common Law had laid down strict rules of Law expressed in archaic terms such as 'consideration' and 'estoppel'. Those strict rules had survived the Judicature Act 1873 and were capable of causing injustice in many cases. There was a gap between those strict rules and the social necessities of the 20th century. The *High Trees* case helped to narrow that gap.

Central London Property Trust Ltd. *vs.* High Trees House Ltd. (1947) KB 130, (1956) 1 All ER 256.

46. Lord Denning, *op. cit.* In the preface, he says:

> My theme is that the principles of law laid down by the judges in the 19th century – however suited to social conditions of that time – are not suited to the social necessities and social opinion of the 20th century. They should be moulded and shaped to meet the needs and opinion of today.

Lord Denning has said words to the same effect in the case of the Attorney-General *v.* Butterworth (1963) 1 QB 696:

> 'It may be that there is no authority to be found in the books, but if this to be to, all I can say is that the sooner we make one the better.'

(Cited in his Due Process of Law, London, 1980, p. 20.)

47. Jerome Frank, Law and the Modern Mind, New York, 1931, pp. 133, 134.

Notes to Chapter 2. A Question of Confidence

2.1 Legal Realism and Legal Certainty

1. See generally W. Twining, Karl Llewellyn and the Realist Movement, London 1973; H. Laswell and M. McDougal, Criteria for a Theory About Law, 44 Southern California Law Review (1971), 362, pp. 371-374.

2. The oracular theory fosters an image of judges as oracles who discover the law's technical mysteries, but who cannot influence the content of law itself. *Cf.* G. Edward White, The American Judicial Tradition, Profiles of Leading American Judges, Oxford, 1978, p. 8. See also Jerome Frank, Law and the Modern Mind, New York, 1931, p. 32; and Felix S. Cohen, Transcendental Nonsense and the Functional Approach, 35 Columbia Law Review (1935), 809.
3. See also M. McDougal, Jurisprudence for a Free Society, 1 Georgia Law Review (1966), 1, at pp. 17-19; J. Paust, The Concept of Norm: A Consideration of the Jurisprudential View of Hart, Kelsen, and McDougal-Laswell, 52 Temple Law Quarterly (1979), 9 at pp. 11-24, 26-27, 31, *passim*; Cohen, Transcendental Nonsense, *op. cit.*
4. Professor Paust has a positive outlook on this feeling of uncertainty. *Cf.* his Concept of Norm, p. 14, n. 17.
5. Alexander M. Bickel, The Least Dangerous Branch, The Supreme Court at the Bar of Politics, New York, 1962, p. 82.
6. Edmond Cahn, Skepticism in American Jurisprudence, in: Confronting Injustice, Ed. Leonore L. Cahn, London, 1967 p. 269. See for a sound evaluation of Legal Realism: Edgar Bodenheimer, Jurisprudence, Cambridge, Mass., 1978, pp. 111-134 and also: Julius Stone, Legal Systems and Lawyers' Reasoning, Stanford, 1964, *passim*.
7. *Cf.* Twining, *op. cit.*; K. Llewellyn, Some Realism about Realism, 44 Harvard Law Review (1931), 1222. (Reprinted, *inter alia*, in: Lord Lloyd of Hampstead, Introduction to Jurisprudence, 1972, pp. 441 *seq.*).
8. *Cf.*, *e.g.* Roscoe Pound, Law in Books and Law in Action, 44 American Law Review (1910), pp. 12 *seq.*
9. Oliver Wendell Holmes, The Path of the Law, in: Collected Legal Papers, New York, 1920, pp. 167-203.
10. *Cf.* Jerome Frank, Law and the Modern Mind, *op. cit.*, p. 102.
11. *Cf.*, *e.g.*, Cohen, *op. cit.*; Twining, *op. cit.*
12. See also Cohen, *op. cit.*; Holmes, *op. cit.*
13. Of course, rule scepticism and fact scepticism are illuminating for trial court *and* upper court level. The bipartition is merely a matter of emphasis.

14. John Thibaut and Laurens Walker, Procedural Justice, A Psychological Analysis, Hillsdale, New York, 1975, pp. 28-41.
15. *Cf.*, *e.g.*, H.L.A. Hart, The Concept of Law, Oxford, 1961, p. 12.
16. Ronald Dworkin, Taking Rights Seriously, London, 1977, pp. 134-136.
17. *Cf.* Bickel, *op. cit.*, p. 16.
18. A vivid description is given by Julian Prescot, Both Sides of the Case, London, 1958, p. 168.
19. See also Cohen, *op. cit.*; McDougal, Jurisprudence for a Free Society, *op. cit.*
20. See for a bibliography: Psychology, Law and Legal Process, Ed. by David P. Farrington, Keith Hawkins and Sally Lloyd-Bostock, London, 1979.
21. *Cf.* Paust, The Concept of Norm, *op. cit.*, pp. 14-18, 26, 31 and 43-44.
22. *Cf.* Max Black, Probability, in: The Encyclopedia of Philosophy, New York, 1972, volume 6, pp. 464-479; Irving M. Copi, Introduction to Logic, London, 1971, third edition, chapter 14, Probability, pp. 419-439.
23. Max Black, *op. cit.*, p. 477.
24. Max Black, *op. cit.*, p. 474.
25. Jerome Frank, *op. cit.*, *passim*. Professor Paust's Concept of Norm, *op. cit.*, is critical of this whining for legal certainty, too. (*Cf.* pp. 14-18, 31 and 43-44.)
26. David W. Rohde and Harold J. Spaeth, Supreme Court Decision Making, San Francisco, 1976.
27. Rohde and Spaeth, *op. cit.*, p. 146.
28. Rohde and Spaeth, *op. cit.*, p. 150.
29. Mr Justice Frank, *In re* Linahan, 138 F. 2d 650, 652 (2d Cir. 1943). Quoted from Walter Gellhorn and Clark Byse, Administrative Law, New York, 1974, p. 945.
30. *Cf.* Rohde and Spaeth, *op. cit.*, chapter 9, The Formation of the Majority Opinion Coalition, pp. 193-210.
31. Albert A. Harrison, Individuals and Groups, Understanding Social Behavior, California, 1976, chapter 10, Performance in Small Groups, p. 447. The lines following the words 'First' and 'Second' are roughly copied from this work.
32. *Cf.* Rohde and Spaeth, *op. cit.*, chapter 9, The Formation

of the Majority Opinion Coalition, pp. 193-207. The topic of coalition formation becomes of special importance in those situations where there is a 'threat to the court', *e.g.* the School Desegregation Cases and the Watergate Tape Case (*op. cit.*, pp. 200-203). See also Bob Woodward and Scott Armstrong, The Brethren, Inside the Supreme Court, New York, 1979, *passim*.

33. Rohde and Spaeth, *op. cit.*, pp. 39-46.
34. *Cf.* Ilmar Tammelo, Modern Logic in the Service of Law, New York, 1978.
35. *E.g.* Ch. Perelman and L. Olbrechts-Tyteca, The New Rhetoric, A Treatise on Argumentation, Notre Dame, Indiana, 1971.
36. Thibaut and Walker, *passim*.
37. *Cf.* Benjamin N. Cardozo, The Nature of the Judicial Process, London, 1977, pp. 163-165.
38. *Cf.*, *e.g.*, McDougal, Jurisprudence for a Free Society, *op. cit.*, pp. 16-19.
39. Cardozo, *op. cit.*, p. 165.
40. Spaeth and Rohde, *op. cit.*, p. 60. See also their reference on p. 68, note 25.
41. Philostratus, Lives of the Sophists, translated from the Greek by Wilmer Cave Wright, London, 1968.
42. *Cf.* W.K.C. Guthrie, The Sophists, Cambridge, 1971, p. 179 and also when describing Protagoras, pp. 19, *seq.* and pp. 181-188; Mario Untersteiner, The Sophists, Oxford, 1954.
43. *Cf.* Professor A. de Swaan, Uitgaansbeperking en uitgaansangst, inaugurele oratie, Amsterdam, May 28, 1979.
44. See also Jerome Frank, Fate and Freedom, 1945, p. 93; E. Fromm, Escape from Freedom, New York, 1941.
45. Cardozo, *op. cit.*, p. 168.
46. Some fifty-five years later Spaeth and Rohde worked out Cardozo's above observation, *op. cit.*, p. 145. For a related approach to normative content and morality see Paust, The Concept of Norm, *op. cit.*; and McDougal, Jurisprudence for a Free Society, *op. cit.*
47. Gellhorn and Byse, *op. cit.*, p. 946.
48. This conclusion may be drawn from reading G. Edward White, *op. cit.* Professor White describes the judges,

mainly U.S. Supreme Court justices, the time in which they lived and how they made law. He implies that it is the judge rather than the lawgiver who determines what the law is. Arguably, this situation is more likely to occur in common-law, than in civil-law countries. But in the latter, too, the doctrine that the judge is solely 'la bouche de la loi' has been abandoned.

49. In such a case, the decision can also be said to be authoritative. See Paust, *op. cit.*, pp. 32-35 and 46-49.
50. *E.g.* The Impact of Supreme Court Decisions, Ed. by Theodore L. Becker and Malcolm M. Feeley, second edition, London, 1973.
51. *Cf.*, *e.g.*, Paust, *op. cit.*, pp. 14-18, 30-31 and 48-49 n. 164.
52. This statement is, however, wishful thinking. An English judge, Lord Justice Diplock, once said: '(if)... £ 9,000 is the appropriate award for injury done to the plaintiff in this case, then I can only say *the scale of values is wrong, and if that is the law, so much worse for the law*' (italics added). McCarey *v.* Associated Newspapers Ltd. (1965) 2QB 86 at 109, (1964) ALL ER 947 at 960. Cited in Duncan & Neill, Defamation, London, 1978.
53. If legal decisions are not generally and relatively freely obeyed or paid attention to, but nevertheless are enforced, an obedience based upon coercion, as opposed to generally shared acceptation, can lapse into tyranny. See also Paust, *op. cit.*, pp. 34-35, 41 and 46-49; and J. Paust, International Law and Control of the Media: Terror, Repression and the Alternatives, 53 Indiana Law Journal (1978), p. 621.

2.2 Equality, Justice and Freedom

54. *Cf.* Rohde and Spaeth, *op. cit.*, pp. 1, 30, 31.
55. Rohde and Spaeth, *op. cit.*, p. 31.
56. Dworkin, *op. cit.*, p. 227.
57. Stanley I. Benn, Equality, Moral and Social, in: The Encyclopedia of Philosophy, *op. cit.*, Volume 3, p. 41.
58. Stanley I. Benn, *op. cit.*, p. 41.
59. Popper, *op. cit.*, Volume II, p. 234.
60. Popper, *op. cit.*, Volume I, p. 89.

61. Ch. Perelman, The Idea of Justice and the Problem of Argument, London, 1970, p. 12.
62. Perelman, *op. cit.*, p. 6.
63. Perelman, *op. cit.*, p. 16.
64. *Cf.* Perelman, *op. cit.*, p. 32.
65. *Cf.* Ilmar Tammelo, Zur Philosophie des Überlebens, Munich, 1975.
66. Bickel, *op. cit.*, p. 27.
67. U.S. Supreme Court, Case No. 76-811. Regents of the University of California *v.* Bakke. Decision of 28 June, 1978.
68. *Cf.* Time Magazine, 10 June, 1978, p. 19. In an article on pp. 18-25 'Bakke Wins, Quotas Lose' Time reported reactions of, *inter alia*, the litigants, members of the legal profession and leaders of interested parties, such as pressure groups. Few were happy with the decision; most found it acceptable.

Notes to Chapter 3. A Question of Concern

3.1 The Bench at the Bar of Politics

1. It is a truism that the meaning of 'political' and 'politics' is a matter of definition. In this chapter, these words are used in their commonsense meaning and not in the meaning of a particular political theory. *Cf.* Peter Laslett and Philip W. Cummings, The History of Political Philosophy, in: The Encyclopedia of Philosophy, *op. cit.*, Volume 6, pp. 370-387.
2. Alexander Bickel has worked this out in his study, 'The Least Dangerous Branch', New York, 1962, pp. 254 *seq.*, especially p. 268. The title of this section is borrowed from the subtitle of this book (*sc.* The Supreme Court at the Bar of Politics).
3. *Cf.* Robert H. Jackson, The Struggle for Judicial Supremacy, New York, 1941.
4. *Cf.* Rohde and Spaeth, *op. cit.*, pp. 201-203; nt. 31 on p. 209.

5. Pericles in his funeral oration when speaking about democracy. Thucydides, Book II, Chapter XXXVI, translated by C.F. Smith, London/Cambridge, Mass., 1951, p. 323.
6. William Sacksteder, Spinoza on Democracy, p. 117, in: Spinoza, Essays in Interpretation, Ed. by Eugene Freeman and Maurice Mandelbaum, Open Court, La Salle, Illinois, 1975.
7. Alasdair MacIntyre; Spinoza, Benedict (Baruch) in: The Encyclopedia of Philosophy, New York 1972, Volume 7, p. 541. Here no political theory will be developed to elaborate the concept of democracy. It will be assumed that the democracies, to be found in countries of Western origin, are the most suitable forms of government - for those countries that is. They guarantee basic rights to individuals and provide a setting in which the individual may try to live his life as he pleases. Needless to say, democracy often falls short of its own ideals. For instance, political power in the Western democracies is quite often political opportunism with insufficient feedback to the will of the majority of the people. Plato suggested that many problems originating from a democratic form of government could be remedied if men of wisdom were in charge. Bertrand Russell retorted to this:

   > It might be suggested that men could be given political wisdom by a suitable training. But the question would arise: What is a suitable training? And this would turn out to be a party question. The problem of finding a collection of 'wise' men and leaving the government to them is thus an insoluble one. That is the ultimate reason for democracy.

   (Bertrand Russell, History of Western Philosophy, London, 1974, p. 124.)
   Proposals for improvement of a democratic form of government have been offered from many sides. Some proposals would have such far-reaching consequences that, carried out, we would lose institutions which are generally considered as essentials of democracy, such as Parliament, human rights. (*cf.*, *e.g.*, Ilmar Tammelo,

Von der Demokratie und darüber hinaus, Umrisse einer 'eurokratischen' Regierungsform, in: Gerd-Klaus Kaltenbrunner, Rückblick auf die Demokratie, Gibt es Alternativen?, Munich, 1977, pp. 96-106.) In theory, there may be better forms of government than a democracy can offer. I see none of them imminent. Moreover, I think that it is dangerous even to touch the fundamentals of democracy. The question how to overhaul and transcend the shortcomings of democracy will be discussed in a limited way only. It can be admitted that Western democracies have their flaws. But that is not the topic of this study. The assumption that a democracy is the most acceptable form of government is taken for granted.

8. Thucydides, *op. cit.*, Chapter XXXVII, pp. 323, 324.
9. Karl R. Popper, The Open Society and Its Enemies, Volume I, The Spell of Plato, Princeton, 1971, pp. 109-110.
10. Popper, *op. cit.*, p. 113.
11. Popper, *op. cit.*, p. 125.
12. Popper, *op. cit.*, p. 121.
13. Popper, *op. cit.*, p. 113.
14. Europe 2000, Ed. Peter Hall, London, 1977, especially pp. 242, *seq.*
15. According to Popper, *op. cit.*, p. 186.
16. Europe 2000, *op. cit., idem.* For the sake of readability no quotation marks are used, although some sentences in this paragraph are quotations.
17. Popper, *op. cit.*, p. 171.
18. G.J. Wiarda, Drie typen van rechtsvinding, Zwolle, 1972, p. 19 and p. 24.
19. G.J. Wiarda, *op. cit.*, p. 106.
20. It is assumed that not only the state may infringe on the individual's basic rights, but also any other powerful organization such as the church, unions, multinational corporations, *etc.* For the sake of simplicity, only the state will be mentioned hereinafter.
21. John P. Roch, Courts and Rights, The American Judiciary in Action, New York, 1968, p. 89.
22. The last three sentences are quotations from Franklin D. Roosevelt's message to the House of Representatives dated 5 February 1937, as printed in Justice Robert H.

Jackson's The Struggle for Judicial Supremacy, New York, 1941, pp. 328, *seq*.

23. An *arrêt de règlement* is a general rule which is not based on a particular case, but makes clear how the court will decide legal matters in the future. If an *arrêt de règlement* cannot be issued, the court always has to wait until a case is presented to the bar. In a court decision, there is a *ratio decidendi*, which may have the force of a precedent that is more or less binding for the future. Judicial decisions may also contain general considerations and rules. The *ratio decidenci* and *obiter dicta* form the 'added value' of a judicial decision. *Cf.* H.U. Jessurun d'Oliveira, De meerwaarde van rechterlijke uitspraken, Arrêts de règlement en precedenten, Deventer, 1973.
24. See his: Taking Rights Seriously, London, 1977, Chapter 5, Constitutional Cases, pp. 131-149.
25. Dworkin, *op. cit.*, pp. 137 *seq*.
26. Dworkin, *op. cit.*, p. 137.
27. Dworkin, *op. cit.*, p. 137.
28. *Cf.* Walter Laqueur, Terrorism - a Balance Sheet, in: The Terrorism Reader, A Historical Anthology, Ed. by Walter Laqueur, New York, 1978, pp. 251-267.
29. *Ex parte* Merryman, 17 Fed. Cas. 144, 153; Case No. 9, 487 as quoted by Robert H. Jackson, The Struggle for Judicial Supremacy, *op. cit.*, p. 326.
30. Henry G. Schermers, The European Court of Justice; Promoter of European Integration, The American Journal of Comparative Law; 1974, pp. 444-464.
31. Idem, pp. 462, 463; Stauder Case (29/69), 12 November 1969, 15 Jur. 425 (1969).
32. Schermers, The European Court of Justice, *op. cit.*, p. 463; Handelsgesellschaft Case (11/70), 17 December 1970, 16 Jur. 1134-39 (1970); (1972) CMLR 282-86; CCH p. 7424 (translation from CCH).
33. Case 23/68, Reports of Cases before the Court (1969), p. 50.
34. Joined Cases 18 and 35/65: Max Gutmann v. Commission of the EAEC, Reports of Cases before the Court (1966), pp. 103, *seq*.
35. Case 41/69: ACF Chemiefarma N.V. v. Commission of the European Communities, Reports of Cases before the

Court (1970), pp. 661, *seq.*

36. *Cf.* Henry G. Schermers, The Communities under the European Convention on Human Rights, Legal Issues of European Integration, 1978/1, pp. 1-8.
37. Henry G. Schermers, The European Court of Justice, *op. cit.*, pp. 452, 453.
38. Henry G. Schermers, The Communities under the European Convention on Human Rights, *op. cit.*.
39. It should be noted that, theoretically the European Court of Human Rights in Strasbourg may fulfil the same task as that which should be granted the Court of Justice in Luxemburg. But in addition to the problems arising from the assignment of this task to either court, the Strasbourg Court faces the disadvantage that its jurisdiction may be limited by the governments of the nations accepting the authority of the Strasbourg Court. The Luxemburg Court is more embedded in the legal systems of the Member States. Its permanent standing enables the Luxemburg Court to take immediate actions when required.

Notes to Chapter 4. A Different Viewpoint

4.1 An Inventory of the Judge's Equipment

1. David Pannock, Fellow of All Souls College, Oxford, in: The Guardian, 10 September, 1979: 'Time to end this English amateur law making'.
2. Pannock *idem.*
3. *Cf.* Anthony Lewis, The Profession of Law, in: International Herald Tribune, July 28, 1971. Mr Lewis contends that the capacity of the American legal system to frame political questions into legal ones make lawyers achieve what social reformers, politicians and union leaders do in other countries. Lewis adds that American law schools are an infinitely greater source of public ideas and public servants than English ones. Although the author of this study is not familiar with either type of law school, he ventures to express some doubts concerning the truth of Mr Lewis' observation. It may be admitted,

though, that De Tocqueville's above observation seems right (*sc.* that of politics legalized).

4. These obvious suggestions were made in a remarkable account in Time Magazine August 20, 1979, of contemporary public perception of judicial performance in the U.S. On pp. 40-46 an article by Evan Thomas and Raissa Silverman was printed under the title 'Judging the Judges'.
5. It must be emphasized that the mere elimination of juries is an amputation of a legal system and – this is important – a possible obstruction of the average Englishman's and American's sense of justice provided by the jury system. Heaven forbid that the jury system should be reintroduced on the continent. But it does have some good aspects. The solution might be to reduce the number of cases in which trial by jury is possible. Incidentally, according to the Administration of Justice Act of 1933 only in seven types of civil action can the parties insist on trial by jury (*i.e.* fraud, defamation and slander, breach of promise of marriage, false imprisonment, malicious prosecution and seduction). This reduction is regarded to be an improvement. (*Cf.* Richard du Cann, Q.C., The Art of the Advocate, Harmondsworth, 1980.)
6. Admittedly, studies and statistics with respect to the cause of delay are scant and not without ambiguity. The same holds for studies relating to the time the district courts take to decide a case, compared to the time spent when decided through arbitration. It is significant, though, that the District Court of Amsterdam has been faster in deciding cases since it adopted a policy of keeping rigid time schedules for lawyers to submit papers and evidence to the court.

4.3 A Plea for the President

7. Adformatie, February 1, 1979, pp. 14-17. This implies an audience of 5 million in a population of 14 million. *Cf.* H. Sleeuwenhoek in the TV programme called 'De Wereld van het Nieuws' (The World of News) NCRV, Nederland 1, February 24, 1979, at 21.55 hours. For this article transcripts were used of the three programmes on gossip magazines and columns broadcast on 2 December, 1978,

24 February, 1979 and 1 March, 1979. The transcript of the first programme was published by Reporterservice, Haarlem. The transcripts of the other two programmes were published by the NCRV Broadcasting Company itself.

8. W. Verstappen, NRC/Handelsblad, 9 March, 1979.
9. Mr. G.E. Langemeijer, De bescherming van eer en goede naam in ons land, N.J.B. 1961, p. 90. In an article in the 'Volkskrant' of 3 March, 1979, K.J. Kraan and R.S. Meijer wrote that there were very few criminal prosecutions for libel: only twenty cases a year, while only a hundred complaints are lodged *per annum*. Incidentally, the author owes an apology to the reader who is not from the continent of Europe. In the Anglo-American legal systems, jurists do not care a button about the writings of a law professor. In the Netherlands, legal disputes may be settled not by reference to a rule of law as laid down by the upper courts, but by oracular pronouncement from a law school. Hence, to persuade the reader originating from the Netherlands, it is advisable to evaluate the doctrine as laid down by law professors, to quote those authorities, to disagree with others in a deferential manner, and then present the point at issue.
10. J.M. de Meij, De vrijheid en verantwoordelijkheid van de pers, Utrecht, 1975. One handicap affecting the task of the Council for Journalists is the fact that there is no obligation for a journalist to appear before the Council. The latter has no sanctions, but the proceedings take a lot of time. De Meij, too, finds criminal law ineffective.
11. Prof. Mr E.M. Meijers, Het Kort Geding, Zwolle, 1945. The translation is not literal. The archaic way in which Dutch legal scholars usually write can be translated into German, but not into English.
12. *Cf.* Judicial statistics of the Central Bureau of Statistics. See for Amsterdam: 1976:653; 1977:712; 1978:812.
13. Mr. W.J. Borgerhoff Mulder, lecture before the Junior Bar Association of Amsterdam, held on 16 November 1977. Source: Jonge Balie Bulletin 1977.
14. Dr. Mr. W. Schenk, Het Kort Geding en Zijn Toepassing in Nederland, Deventer, 1976, p. 58. The translation is not literal.

15. *Idem*, pp. 58, 59. The translation is not literal.
16. This is a fine example of the oracular theory.
17. This circular reasoning is also a nice example of Transcendental Nonsense.
18. *Op. cit.*
19. Prof. Mr. W.H. Heemskerk, note under H.R. 2 April 1976, N.J. 1977, 361. He quotes with appreciation Mr. N. Okma, preadvies H.N.J.V., 1950, I, who also argues that a summary proceeding may result in a declaratory judgment.
20. Hugenholtz-Heemskerk, Hoofdlijnen van Nederlands Burgerlijk Procesrecht, Den Haag, 1976, p. 111. This change of Heemskerk was discovered by Mr. A.P. Funke, N.J.B., 1977, pp. 1119, 1120. Funke agrees with Heemskerk's latest opinion.
21. Unfortunately, the courts of appeal do not publish statistics relating to their dockets. But it may be safely assumed that no more than a tenth of the judgments of the President of the District Court of Amsterdam are appealed against and that the Court of Appeal of Amsterdam reverses at most a quarter of the cases. That implies a 2 to 3% quota of reversed judgements.
22. On the Continent, the courts usually give judgment in the manner of, for instance, the U.S. Court. (Or is it *vice versa*?) They never give judgment directly after the hearing.
23. In the Netherlands there is no common law principle of *stare decisis*. Nevertheless, precedents are not totally ignored. *Cf.* President of the District Court of Den Bosch, 4 February 1949, N.J. 1950, 183. The President rules that this is, in fact, payment of alimony. His decision does not prejudice other proceedings since plaintiff is in the position to repay what she receives, if necessary.
    President of the District Court of Zutphen, 9 November 1950, N.J. 1951, 209. There is already a decision of the court ruling that defendant is liable. Now there is a litigation pending regarding the height of damages. Plaintiff has no source of income and her financial situation is desperate.
    President of the District Court of Groningen June 17, 1953, N.J. 1954, 33. Payment of an advance is ordered,

because there is a duty to pay alimony.
Court of Appeal of Arnhem, June 16, 1959, N.J., 1960, 300. The President was right when he ordered a weekly payment after presuming that defendant was liable.
Court of Appeal of Amsterdam, September 20, 1960, V.R. 1961, 85. The President was right to order payment of an advance when plaintiff was badly hurt in an accident and has no source of income, whereas defendant is probably liable.
President of the District Court of Haarlem, June 26, 1962, N.J. 1963, 161. Defendant cannot reasonably deny liability. The President assumes authority to pay an advance, even if non-payment does not put the plaintiff in a situation of emergency.

24. That is obvious in for instance, orders for the eviction of squatters. Those orders are always final.
25. *Cf.* Ronald Dworkin, Taking Rights Seriously, London, 1977, chapters 4 and 5, especially pp. 134 *seq.*
26. *Cf.* Gatley on Libel and Slander, London, 1974, pp. 556-570, and first supplement to the seventh edition, 1979, paragraph 1359, 1368. See also Duncan & Neill, Defamation, London, 1978, pp. 130-145.
27. Edmond Cahn, The Consumers of Injustice, lecture delivered in 1959, in: Confronting Injustice, ed. by Lenore L. Cahn, London, 1967, pp. 10 *seq.*
28. *Cf.* Alexander M. Bickel, The Supreme Court and the Idea of Progress, New Haven and London, 1979, p. 81.
29. Bickel, *op. cit.*, p. 94.

Notes to Chapter 5. Discretion

5.1 Legal Limitations to Discretion

1. *Cf.* for a general discourse on 'discretion': Julius Stone, Legal System and Lawyers' Reasonings, Stanford, 1964, Chapter 7, Categories of Illusory Reference in the Growth of the Common Law, pp. 235-300. See also the classic on 'freies Ermessen': Rudolf von Laun, Das freie Ermessen und seine Grenzen Leipzig-Vienna, 1910; Kurt Ringhofer, Strukturprobleme des Rechts, Vienna,

1960, pp. 22 *seq.*, 33 *seq.*; and recently: Horst Ehmke, 'Ermessen' und 'unbestimmte Rechtsbegriff' im Verwaltungsrecht, Tübingen, 1966. In this chapter only the concept of discretion will be discussed, not its various conceptions.

2. H.L.A. Hart, The Concept of Law, Oxford, 1961, p. 141.
3. *idem.*
4. Hart, *op. cit.*, pp. 141, 142.
5. Hart, *op. cit.*, p. 142.
6. Edgar Bodenheimer, Hart, Dworkin, and the problem of Judicial Lawmaking Discretion, in: Georgia Law Review, 11 (1977), p. 1162.
7. Bodenheimer, *op. cit.*, p. 1163.

5.3 Courts and Corporations

8. The translation of this preamble is not literal. *Cf.* Bijlage Handelingen Tweede Kamer (House of Representatives), 1967-1968, 9596.
9. The 'Sociaal Economische Raad' is an advisory body to the Government. One third of its members are appointed by professional organizations of entrepreneurs, one third by unions and one third by the Government.
10. Mr. Polak is a member of the Conservative Party (that is, V.V.D.).
11. The translation of Mr Polak's speech, which fills the rest of paragraph 2.3.2, is not literal. *Cf.* Handelingen Eerste Kamer (Senate), 1969-1970, 1095.
12. By 'independence' is meant formal, legal and 'institutional' independence. This is something quite different from personal independence. There is a lot of discussion about this subject at the present time. As a judge is not a machine, but a human being, he has certain attitudes that influence the outcome of court cases. See chapter 2.1 Legal Realism and Legal Certainty. For the sake of reasoning in this chapter, personal independence is taken for granted: it is assumed that the judge is able to render fair – that is, objective and impartial – decisions.
13. *Cf.* former Attorney-General at the Dutch Supreme Court Dr. G.E. Langemeijer in HR. 17 April 1959, N.J. 1961-573. See for literature and precedents: Onrechtma-

tige Daad VII, Drion c.s., Special Liability, nr. 147-158.

14. Article 2.346 of the Dutch Civil Code. The Amsterdam Attorney-General may also request this investigation (article 2.345 D.C.C.).
15. Article 2.356-2.358 D.C.C.
16. *Cf.* Handelingen Eerste Kamer (Senate) 1969-1970, 1095.
17. Article 2.357, 2.358 section 1 D.C.C.
18. *Cf.* Prof. Mr. P. van Schilfgaarde, Van de naamloze en de besloten vennootschap, Arnhem, 1976, p. 236.
19. *Cf.* Bijlage Handelingen Tweede Kamer (House of Representatives) 1978-1979, nr. 13.394.
20. Article 2.337 D.C.C.
21. *Cf.* Court of Appeal of Amsterdam, 14 April 1979, TVVS 1977-8.
22. *Cf.* Court of Appeal of Amsterdam, April 14, 1977, N.J. 1978-442: The unions are interested parties; Court of Appeal of Amsterdam, 26 May 1977 (S.O.B.I. *v.* Vulkaansoord N.V.): an interested party is a holder of one share only. See also: Rechtspersonen, Deventer, Deel II, Titel 6, De jaarrekening, door Mr Th.S. IJsselmuiden, commentaar op art. 2.337 B.V., aant. 7.
23. President of the District Court of The Hague, 21 December 1950, N.J. 1951-70. *Cf.* D.J. Veegens, in: J.M. van Dunné *et al.*, Acht Civilisten in Burger, Zwolle, 1977, pp. 266-269.
24. The Council of State is an advisory body to the Government, especially with regard to new legislation. Its origin goes back to the Middle Ages. Recently, the Council has been extended by a Judicial Division that is the highest administrative court in the Netherlands. (The former Judicial Division did not have the broad jurisdiction of the present one.)
25. Afdeling Rechtspraak, Raad van State, 16 September 1978. Weekoverzicht Raad van State, Bijvoegsel Nederlandse Staatscourant, Afdeling Rechtspraak.
26. R.M. Dworkin, Taking Rights Seriously, London, 1977, chapter 4, Hard Cases, chapter 5, Constitutional Cases. See in particular pp. 134 *seq*.
27. The author disagrees with Professor Dworkin regarding, *inter alia*, the notion of discretion. See chapter 1.3.5 Discretion.

28. *Cf.* Dworkin, *op. cit.*

29. The Enterprise Chamber of the Amsterdam Court of Appeal has original jurisdiction. Appeal to the Supreme Court is possible only for complaints of improper ruling regarding the *law*. Judgments of the Courts of Appeal are immune insofar as what the *facts* are. The decision as to whether mismanagement has taken place or not is one of fact. (The Supreme Court considers only whether the law has been properly applied. It must assume that the Court of Appeal has stated the facts correctly.)

30. *Cf.* Handelingen Eerste Kamer 1969-1970, 1093, 1094. Mr. Polak expressed this opinion in a hilarious speech against a senator who, being a law professor, asked the Minister questions which made clear that he was unfamiliar with even the legal principles that every undergraduate knows by heart. To use a variation of a saying of Clarence Darrow: When I was a child, I was told that every man could become a senator; I am beginning to believe it.

31. The Supreme Court even ignored even the instruction that some legal rules cannot be overruled: HR March 3, 1972, N.J., 1972-339; HR 1 May 1924; N.J. 1924-684.

32. This is a concept without a denotation, but with a connotation only.

33. Prof. Mr. Paul Scholten, Algemeen Deel, Asser-serie, Zwolle, 1954, Second Edition, catch 19.

34. Dr. G.E. Langemeijer, the former Attorney-General at the Dutch Supreme Court, headed a study group in Amsterdam consisting of law professors, judges, some advocates and other jurists. The study group dissolved when Dr. Langemeijer retired. Dr.Langemeijer used the term 'legal conscience' at the session of 7 October 1977 to refer to the tendency to operate with and within the legal system.

5.4 Psychological and Moral Limitations Discretion

35. C.G. Jung Speaking, Interviews and Encounters, Ed. William McGuire and R.F.C. Hull, The Houston Films, Second Interview, London, 1978, p. 297.

36. Dr. J. Jacobi, Die Psychologie von C.G. Jung, Zürich, 1945, pp. 41, 42.

37. Krech, Crutchfield, Ballachey, Individual in Society, New York, 1962, pp. 500 *seq.*
38. Rod A. Bond and Nigel F. Lemon, Changes in Magistrates' Attitudes During the First Year on the Bench, in: Psychology, Law and Legal Process, Ed. David P. Farrington, Keith Hawkins and Sally Lloyd-Bostock, London, 1979, pp. 125 *seq.* The conclusion is that the magistrates' initial views are susceptible to influence from training and experience. Changes tend to be induced in viewpoints on the more procedural aspects of a magisstrate's work and on sentencing matters rather than in the potentially more deep-seated views on penal philosophy and policy.
39. David W. Rohde and Harold J. Spaeth, Supreme Court Decision Making, San Francisco, 1976, pp. 24, 25.
40. *Cf.* Charles A. Kiesler and Sara B. Kiesler, Conformity, Reading, Mass., 1970, pp. 11, 12.
41. Jerome Frank, Law and the Modern Mind, Norwood, Mass., 1931, part three, chapter II, Mr. Justice Oliver Wendell Holmes, The Completely Adult Jurist, pp. 253 *seq.*
42. René König, The Restless Image, A Sociology of Fashion, London, 1973, p. 34.
43. König, *op. cit.*, p. 32.

Notes to Chapter 6. Logic and 'New' Rhetoric

6.1 Life of Law is Experience, Not Logic

1. Oliver Wendell Holmes, The Common Law, 1881, reprinted in 1968, London, p. 1.
2. Felix S. Cohen in: L.K. Cohen, ed., The Legal Conscience, Selected Papers of Felix S. Cohen, New Haven, 1960, pp. 25, 26. Quoted from A. Bickel, The Least Dangerous Branch, New York, 1960, pp. 79, 80.
3. Lawrence J. Smith, Art of Advocacy, New York, 1978. This loose-leaf edition suggests possibilities for influencing court occupants. A lawyer can become a shyster by applying these. At the same time, as argued in chapter 6.2, there are gross risks involved in the use of unethical

methods. By and large, they may produce favourable results occasionally, but are unattractive when practised as a habit. A lawyer's reputation is decisive for his income. The majority of the members of the bar can best survive if they merely take the trouble to avoid tarnishing their reputation.

4. Aristotle, 'Art' of Rhetoric, translated by John Henry Freese, London, 1947. (Loeb Series.)

6.2 Legal Reasoning at Bar

5. Ilmar Tammelo, Modern Logic in the Service of Law, Vienna-New York, 1978.
6. Tammelo, *op. cit.*, pp. 149-156.
7. Tammelo, *op. cit.*, p. 2.
8. Tammelo, *op. cit.*, p. 3.
9. Tammelo, *op. cit.*, p. 3.
10. Tammelo, *op. cit.*, pp. 153-154.
11. Tammelo, *op. cit.*, p. 152.
12. Tammelo, *op. cit.*, p. 155.
13. *Cf.* Ambrose Bierce, The Devil's Dictionary, in: The Collected Writings of Ambrose Bierce, New Jersey, 1972, p. 289. See for a more balanced judgement regarding the essentials of advocacy: Richard du Cann, Q.C., The Art of the Advocate, Harmondsworth, 1980, p. 47.
14. Bierce, *op. cit.*, p. 289.

6.3 A Logical Scrutiny of the Van Duyn Case

15. Van Duyn *v.* Home Office, Judgment of 4.12.1974, Case 41/74, The European Court of Justice, Reports of the Cases before the Court, 1974, Part II, pp. 1337-1359.
16. See, for instance, I. Tammelo, Modern Logic in the Service of Law, 1978, Vienna-New York, pp. 110-118.
17. *Ibid*, p. vii.
18. See *op. cit. supra* n. 2; I. Tammelo & H. Schreiner, Grundzüge und Grundverfahren der Rechtslogik Münich (vol. I 1974, vol. II 1977); I. Tammelo & G. Moens, Logische Verfahren der Juristischen Begründung, Vienna-New York, 1976.
19. See *e.g.* J. Esser, Grundsatz und Norm in der richterlich-

ten Fortbildung des Privatrechts, Tübingen, 1965, p. 221.

20. See *e.g.* H. Kelsen, Recht und Logik, 19 Neues Forum, 1965, pp. 421 ff.
21. Cited *supra* n. 2.
22. See especially *op. cit. supra* n. 2, pp. 9-21, 55-62. A proof of the completeness of the counter-formula method has been provided in P. Lorenzen, 'Die Vollständigkeit einer unverzweigten Variante des 'analytischen' Entscheidungsverfahrens der klassischen Logik' 18 Archiv für mathematische Logik und Grundlagenforschung, 1976, pp. 19-22.
23. Comprised in D.J. Gijlstra *et al.* (eds.), Leading Cases and Materials on the Law of the European Communities, Deventer, (2nd ed. 1977), p. 202 ff.
24. This rule is an addition to the logical equipment of the counterformula method. Its application would considerably expedite the application of this method in certain cases. Dr. Schreiner is preparing an article on the rule.

6.4 A Complementary Scrutiny of the Van Duyn Case

25. *Cf.* W.R. Böhning, The Migration of Workers in the United Kingdom and the European Community, Oxford, 1972, especially pp. 72-77.
26. Lord Denning has come to the same conclusion that the Court has taken policy consideration into account. He also said that the Van Duyn case is a good illustration of the way in which the European Court interprets the Treaty and the Directives. See his *The Due Process of Law*, London, 1980, p. 166.
27. *Cf.*, for example, R.Ch. Goffin, J.T. 4903, pp. 154-155; R.H. Lauwaars, S.E.W. 1976, pp. 74-83; H. Rittstieg, Eur. 1976, pp. 54-58; I. Telchini, Riv.Dir. Int. Priv. e Proc., 1975, N.2, p. 394; D.J. Devine, Ir. Jur. 1974, pp. 294-316; D. Wyatt, Eur. L. Rev., 1975, pp. 64-67; P. Allott, Camb. L.J. 1976, pp. 3-6; D. Wyatt, Eur. L. Rev., 1975, pp. 51-53; K.R. Simons, Int. Comp. L.Q., 1975, pp. 419-437; G. Lyon-Caen, Rev. trim. dr. eur., 1976 no. 1, p. 142.
28. Felix S. Cohen, Transcendental Nonsense and the

Functional Approach, In: L.K. Cohen, ed., The Legal Conscience, Selected Papers of F.S. Cohen, New Haven, 1960, pp. 33-76.

29. Cohen, *op. cit.*, p. 45.
30. *Cf.* Cohen, *op. cit.*, p. 52, quoting C.S. Peirce.
31. Cohen, *op. cit.*, pp. 70, 71.

INDEX OF NAMES

INDEX OF SUBJECTS

I am content, necessarily, but not to the point of clapping my hands.

Malone Dies
Samuel Beckett